Roger Shatt
teacher, scholar and critic.
National Book Award in 1
published writings include a number of short stories and
numerous translations. He is the Commonwealth Professor of French at the University of Virginia.

'A strange sad tale, and a fascinating book which not
only tells the story, but critically examines Itard's diagnoses, and his treatment, of the wild boy of Aveyron'
Jayne Gilman, *Oxford Mail*

A 'finely researched, scrupulous account'
Sally Vincent, *New Society*

'Professor Shattuck tells us the whole history of the
"Savage's" dismemberment and attempted re-assembly
. . . he tells it very well'
Nigel Dennis, *Sunday Telegraph*

'No one has ever addressed the issues – of freedom,
humanity, culture, doubt and wonder – with more intelligence and grace'   John Leonard, *New York Times*

ALSO BY ROGER SHATTUCK

Half Tame (poems)
Marcel Proust
*The Banquet Years: The Origins of the Avant-Garde
   in France, 1885 to World War I*

The Forbidden Experiment

The Story of the Wild Boy of Aveyron

Roger Shattuck

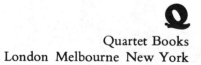

Quartet Books

London Melbourne New York

Published by Quartet Books Limited 1981
A member of the Namara Group
27/29 Goodge Street, London W1P 1FD

First published in Great Britain in hardcover by
Secker and Warburg Ltd, London, 1980

ISBN 0 7043 3383 X

Made and printed in Great Britain by
Lowe & Brydone Ltd., Leeds, Yorkshire

British Library Cataloguing in Publication Data

Shattuck, Roger
   The forbidden experiment.
   1.   Victor, *of Aveyron*
   2.   Feral children
   I.   Title
   155.4'5'670924   GN 372

ISBN 0–7043–3383–X

FOR
Eileen
Patricia
Marc
Tari

Contents

vii

Contents ix

. . . What is a man
If his chief good and market of his time
Be but to sleep and feed? A beast, no more.
Shakespeare, *Hamlet*, IV, 4

The Forbidden Experiment

THE STORY OF THE
WILD BOY OF AVEYRON

Foreword

This is a true story, as true as I can tell it. The story recounts an extraordinary life that was neither good nor evil nor conventionally heroic. The Wild Boy of Aveyron survived on the outer edges of humanity in a state of something like moral weightlessness. We have no need to pass judgment on him, only to take account of so remarkable a case. The appeal of the story lies in a rare combination of uncertainty and hope lodged in the events themselves, and in the way those events seem to touch our own lives.

The story includes two other people: a young doctor who became both a central character and the principal witness, and a woman whose devotion in many ways surpassed his. The events the doctor recorded illuminate, but do not dispel, the mysteries of human nature and human culture. The life of the Wild Boy of Aveyron, who was once the talk of Europe, is at the same time a true story and a mystery story.

Little wonder that the events have led to conflicting interpretations. Psychology, biology, history, sociology, linguistics, anthropology, philosophy—all these areas of knowledge and inquiry have a contribution to make to our understanding of the case. When the time comes, I shall speak of them. But chiefly this book offers a straightforward narrative account of the boy who was briefly called Joseph and later called Victor. During his lifetime, most people knew him simply as the "Savage." No one has yet discovered his family name or where he came from originally. But we know the essentials that form the heart of the story. I believe it is worth telling in full.

1

Prisoner without a Crime

(JANUARY TO NOVEMBER 1800)

Out of the Forest

Before dawn on January 9, 1800, a remarkable creature came out of the woods near the village of Saint-Sernin in southern France. No one expected him. No one recognized him. He was human in bodily form and walked erect. Everything else about him suggested an animal. He was naked except for the tatters of a shirt and showed no modesty, no awareness of himself as a human person related in any way to the people who had captured him. He could not speak and made only weird, meaningless cries. Though very short, he appeared to be a boy of about eleven or twelve, with a round face under dark matted hair. During the night he had approached the lower part of the village, where the Rance River leaves a narrow wooded valley and sweeps under a stone bridge. The boy had entered the terraced garden of a tanner and begun digging for vegetables. There the tanner caught him.

From the scanty records that survive, it is hard to tell how vigorously the boy resisted capture. Probably the tanner hardly knew what to do with his strange prisoner. Word of the event spread rapidly through the village and soon reached the local commissioner, a prominent citizen by the name of Constans-Saint-Estève. In an official report written three weeks later, he gives the first eyewitness account. The Wild Boy does not sound completely unaccustomed to people.

The whole neighborhood learned about it quickly and everyone turned out to see the child. People referred to him as a wild savage. I hurried down there myself to make my own decision about how far to believe the stories. I found him sitting by a warm fire, which he seemed to enjoy, but showing signs of uneasiness from time to time, probably because of the great crowd of people around him. For a while I watched him without saying anything. When I spoke to him, it didn't take long to discover that he was mute. Soon after that, when I noticed that he made no response to various questions I put to him, in both a loud and a soft voice, I decided that he must be deaf.

When I took him affectionately by the hand to lead him to my house, he resisted strenuously. But a series of caresses and particularly two hugs I gave him, with a friendly smile, changed his mind, and after that he seemed to trust me.

When we reached my house, I decided he must be hungry . . . To find out what he liked, I had my servant offer him on a big earthenware platter raw and cooked meat, rye and wheat bread, apples, pears, grapes, nuts, chestnuts, acorns, potatoes, parsnips, and an orange. He picked up the potatoes confidently and tossed them into the fire to cook them. One at a time he seized the other items, smelled them, and rejected them . . . With his right hand he picked the potatoes right out of the live coals and ate them roasting hot. There was no way to persuade him to let them cool off a little. He made sharp, inarticulate, yet scarcely complaining sounds that indicated the hot food was burning him. When he got thirsty, he glanced around the room. Noticing the pitcher, he placed my hand in his without any other sign and led me to the pitcher, which he tapped with his left hand as a means of asking for a drink. Some wine was brought, but he scorned it and showed impatience at my delay in giving him water to drink.

When he had finished his frugal meal, he stood up and ran out the door. In spite of my shouts he kept on running, and I had a hard time catching him. When I brought him back, he seemed neither pleased nor displeased. This unfortunate being had already aroused my deepest interest.

> —P.-J. Bonnaterre, *Notice historique sur le sauvage de l'Aveyron*, Paris, 1800.*

Within the first hour or two, Constans, the alert commissioner, must have noticed something else he doesn't mention in this report. The boy was totally "unhousebroken." He relieved himself wherever and whenever he felt like it, squatting to urinate, defecating while standing. Constans must have meditated a long time over "this unfortunate being" and finally came to a conclusion: "From earliest childhood, this boy has lived in the woods, a stranger to social needs and habits."

* All translations are by Roger Shattuck.

From earliest childhood. Constans had no way of knowing how the boy had lived for the past six or eight years. His words suggest that he found this creature's behavior utterly unfamiliar even in a remote village. Yet Constans nowhere mentioned the possibility of the boy being an idiot, even though idiots were a common sight two hundred years ago in such a region. And how does one account for the remains of a shirt?

The villagers of Saint-Sernin crowded around to satisfy their natural curiosity. They saw a boy-animal, an escaped half-wit perhaps, or even a goblin, something subhuman or supernatural. He would have been received that way in almost any village in the world. However, the reactions of Constans went beyond curiosity. The remoteness of Saint-Sernin and the lack of rapid communications would have made it easy for him to ignore or forget the whole affair. After a few days the boy would probably have escaped to the woods again. But Constans was fairly well educated, had read a little science and philosophy, and had traveled to Paris for several months in 1792 to represent his district at republican assemblies after the French Revolution. He was now in charge of the local government. As his letters show, Constans sensed that he was dealing with an unusual specimen, a case which it was his responsibility to record and pass along to higher authorities.

Two days later, the local police transported the still naked boy twenty-five miles to an orphanage, or hospice, in the town of Saint-Affrique. He stayed there almost a month before continuing his journey toward civilization. It is surprising he survived, for at this moment in French history homes for abandoned children were desperately overcrowded, racked by epidemics, and so short of funds they could supply only one meal a day and no coffins.

Father Bonnaterre, Priest and Naturalist

During the time the boy was held in Saint-Affrique, according to one report, the people taking care of him had a name for him: Joseph. It would have been both a convenience and a recognition of his human status, but the name was never recorded or used officially. The boy must have had a spell of depression or sickness in Saint-Affrique, for the reports say he made no sound for two weeks. And they supply a few more details.

> Accustomed to all the hardships of winter in the open air and at a high altitude, the boy wouldn't tolerate any kind of clothing. He pulled his clothes off as soon as he had been dressed, or tore them up if he couldn't get them off . . . When he arrived at the home, he showed a great aversion to sleeping in a bed. However, he gradually got used to doing so, and later on showed his pleasure whenever his sheets were changed.

He continued to sniff all his food suspiciously and to accept almost nothing but potatoes. When he tried a mouthful of white bread, he spat it out immediately. Twice he escaped, and was recaptured with great difficulty. The director of the orphanage and one other witness say they once saw the boy drop to all fours when he was about to be retaken. But the report is unreliable. Usually he ran like an ordinary boy, *"à toutes jambes"*—as fast as his two legs could carry him.

This is the extent of our information on the profound changes the boy must have been going through. Meanwhile, important developments that concerned him were taking place locally and in Paris. Constans-Saint-Estève, the commissioner who first took charge of the boy in Saint-Sernin, sent a letter with him to the orphanage stating that he was probably a deaf-mute. Displaying remarkable knowledge of Paris, Constans wrote that "the government will no doubt decide that this boy should be entrusted to the celebrated and respected Sicard." This ambitious and gifted priest had made an international reputation by training deaf-mute children in sign language and in writing, and as director of the Institute for Deaf-Mutes in Paris. Constans was right; the Abbé Sicard would have an important role in the story.

The director of the orphanage in Saint-Affrique, named Rainaldis Nougairoles, immediately grasped the potential interest of the case both for men of learning and for ordinary citizens. The next day he sat down and composed a letter of his own in which he added further details about the boy's history and habits. Nougairoles asserted that he was not deaf and twice referred to him as a "phenomenon"—for which the government should assume responsibility. He sent Constans's letter and his own to the *Journal des débats* in Paris, where they were published fourteen days later. (See Appendix I.) Thus the news traveled with astonishing speed to Paris and from there to other cities.

Local scholars pricked up their ears immediately. And, naturally, the whole body of ancient mythology about wild men and savages reappeared in the press.

> . . . Stories about the boy were spread through the entire Republic. As usual, the most extraordinary details were added. Some said he was hairy as a bear; others that he swam and dove like a duck; others that he could leap from tree to tree like a squirrel, and so on.
>
> Many papers ran the story. All Paris was buzzing with word of the Savage of Aveyron. But the central administration of the district has still received no official report on the subject.

The man who wrote these words was a priest and naturalist living in Rodez, fifty miles to the north of Saint-Affrique, and capital of the Aveyron district. Pierre-Joseph Bonnaterre had spent the years before the Revolution in Paris, studying and contributing articles on zoology to an encyclopedia. As a member of the Church, Bonnaterre had had to flee from the Terror in Paris back to his birthplace in Aveyron. When calm was restored, his competence and reputation earned him an appointment to the new Central School which the revolutionary government opened in Rodez.

Two weeks after the boy was captured, Bonnaterre went in person to see the Central Commissioner of Aveyron, there in Rodez, and offered to travel to Saint-Affrique to obtain first-hand information on the case. The commissioner took an immediate interest and went even further. He ordered that the boy be brought to Rodez and entrusted to Bonnaterre. About ten days later, on February 4, the boy arrived, "surrounded by an immense crowd that exasperated him so much he bit anyone who came close."

Bonnaterre was not the only person spurred to action by news of the "Aveyron Savage." When Sicard, director of the Institute for Deaf-Mutes in Paris, read or heard about the two letters in the *Journal des débats* in late January 1800, he probably saw a new opportunity to apply his skills. Several children had been brought to him who were considered retarded or idiots; he demonstrated that they were deaf-mutes who could learn to understand and talk through sign language. Public education of the deaf was his mission. Just a month earlier Sicard had helped found the Society of Observers of Man, a scientific association. When he heard about the Wild Boy of Aveyron, Sicard took two energetic steps. He had the head of the new Society write to Saint-Affrique and request custody of the boy for scientific purposes. And by some means he aroused the interest of the new Minister of the Interior, Napoleon's brother. Lucien Bonaparte signed a terse letter to the commissioner in Rodez: "I want the boy here and instruct you to send him without delay."

It could have been a touchy situation. Just after the boy arrived in Rodez and was turned over to Bonnaterre, enormous pressure was put on the commissioner to send the boy on to higher authorities in Paris. The commissioner's answer to the minister was sensible, and perhaps a little self-serving. In careful language, observing full protocol, he requested permission to keep the boy until he had been seen by parents looking for missing children. He also expressed doubts about the authenticity of the case, implying that the affair might be some kind of a hoax that the authorities should not yet make too much of. "It seems certain," the commissioner reported, "that he is not a true savage." But how could he know? Sicard and the Minister of the Interior agreed to wait. The boy spent five and a half months in the Ecole Centrale of Rodez under Bonnaterre's care.

A few anxious parents did show up, but none recognized or claimed the boy. Meanwhile, Bonnaterre was observing everything and taking notes from which he could soon write an account. His description is careful and apparently objective.

> Outwardly, this boy is no different from other boys. He stands four feet one inch tall; he appears to be about twelve or thirteen years old. He has delicate white skin, a round face, long eyelashes, a long, slightly pointed nose, an average-size mouth, a rounded chin, generally agreeable features, and an engaging smile.

Behind his matted hair and outlandish behavior, the boy scarcely had the appearance of a wild man. But Bonnaterre goes on to report that the boy's whole body was covered with scars, which suggested either mistreatment suffered before he was abandoned or the great hardships he survived in the woods.

> When he raises his head, one can see at the upper end of the tracheal artery, right across the glottis, a healed-over wound about an inch and a half long. It looks like the scar left by a sharp instrument. Could some barbarous hand, having led this child into the wilderness, have turned a murderous weapon against him in order to make his disappearance more sure and final?

Some of the boy's lower teeth were a little loose and yellowed, but he had no apparent malformation of the tongue, mouth, or vocal cords to explain his lack of speech. His right leg turned in slightly when he walked, but not seriously. Bonnaterre concluded that there was "no basic flaw in his external makeup." Still, he displayed some strange behavior.

> When he is sitting down, and even when he is eating, he makes a guttural sound, a low murmur; and he rocks his body from right to left or backwards and forwards, with his head and chin up, his mouth closed, and his eyes staring at nothing. In this position he sometimes has spasms, convulsive movements that may indicate that his nervous system has been affected.

After careful consideration, Bonnaterre stated that there was nothing wrong with the boy's five senses but that their order of importance or sensitivity seemed to be modified. He relied first on smell, then on taste; his sense of touch came last. His sight was sharp; his hearing seemed to shut out many sounds people around him paid close attention to. Nothing interested him but food and sleep. Bonnaterre came to the melancholy conclusion that "his desires do not go beyond his physical needs" and that even the fondness the boy developed for the person taking care of him was selfish and reflected no feeling of gratitude.

The person who really took care of the young boy was an old peasant by the name of Clair, the school gardener. Not much is said about Clair, but everything suggests that he saw more of the boy than anyone else during those five months in Rodez. Bonnaterre observed and tested the boy when he had time. Clair filled the multiple roles of jailer, foster parent, servant, and tutor; he spent nearly all day and all night with his charge. As he went about his tasks of feeding and cleaning and dressing the boy, Clair probably talked to him as people talk to a baby or an animal, and tried to train him to do the things a normally brought up boy would do for himself. But we have no record of whether Clair tried any systematic program of reeducation.

Bonnaterre does give us a sketch of the boy's schedule. A light sleeper, he usually woke up at dawn and then lounged about his room, sitting up in bed with a blanket wrapped around his head until breakfast at nine. He went next door to Clair's room to eat roast potatoes, chestnuts or beans, and rye bread, which he apparently accepted. In cold weather, he warmed himself squatting in front of the fire. Sitting in a chair did not begin until later. He went back to his own room until close to noon, when he ate a second meal of soup, bread, and sometimes meat or potatoes. It took him four months to develop a taste for meat, "which he ate raw or cooked, indifferently." His favorite foods were peas, garden beans, and green walnuts. Water was his only drink. When he spilled a little soup on his hands, he dried them not on a cloth but in ashes he scooped out of the fireplace. In good weather he was taken out for a walk on a leash in the early afternoon. He then stayed in his room, lying down until suppertime around six.

When it's time to go to bed, nothing can stop him. He picks up a candlestick, points at the key to his room, and goes into a rage if he is not obeyed.

Each day he eats about two pounds of rye bread and about the same amount of vegetables and potatoes.

His winter clothing consists of a shirt, a jacket, and a short skirt reaching to his knees. He has gone barefoot and bareheaded all winter.

Bonnaterre reports that the boy grew fast in these months and caught only one stubborn cold. "He coughs often and never spits." Very slowly he began to learn to relieve himself not just anywhere (Bonnaterre says he never soiled or wet his bed) but outside in the courtyard.

For Clair, it must have been like living with a monkey. Yet Bonnaterre takes care to describe certain kinds of behavior that might suggest more than mere animality in the boy.

His constant need for food multiplies his connections with the objects around him and develops a certain degree of intelligence in him. During his stay in Rodez his sole occupation consisted of shelling beans, and he performed that job as efficiently as an experienced person. Since he knew that the beans were a regular part of his ration, as soon as he saw a bunch of dried beanstalks he went to get a pot. He set up his work space in the middle of the room, laying out the different articles as conveniently as possible. With the pot at his right and the beanstalks at his left, he opened the pods one after the other with incredible dexterity. The good beans he dropped into the pot, rejecting the mildewed or blackened ones. If one got away from him he kept his eye on it, picked it up, and put it with the others. As he emptied the pods, he set them down next to him in a symmetrical

pile. When he had finished, he picked up the pot, put
water in it, set it on the fire, which he built up by adding
the dry pods. If the fire had gone out, he picked up the
shovel and gave it to Clair, making signs that he should
go find some live coals in the neighborhood. As soon as
the pot began to boil, he demonstrated his desire to eat.
And there was no alternative but to pour the half-cooked
beans into his plate. He ate them eagerly.

Some psychologists today would probably argue that an ape
can be trained to do almost as well. Bonnaterre, however, is
pointing out not only that the boy had learned how to shell
beans but also that he did so with a certain system and care
which seemed particularly intelligent. The boy might *eat* like
an animal, but he *worked* like a rational creature. Does an
untutored child of nature have an inborn sense of order waiting to show itself? Bonnaterre lets the details of this case
speak for themselves. There are several more parables as
straightforward as this one.

The boy was housed during these five months in the
Central School buildings in the town of Rodez. One day
Bonnaterre decided to take him along on a visit to a friend in
the country. A social call did not change the boy's behavior in
the slightest. Only food interested him. For once, he was
offered more than he wanted. When he had eaten enough, he
swept the leftovers into his skirt, went out to the garden, and,
"with a foresight common to animals who may find themselves short of food later on," buried them in the ground. At
home, he became very sly and skillful at pilfering food from
the stove.

Bonnaterre showed the boy a mirror to see how he would
react; it was a standard test for savages and idiots. He apparently saw a person but did not recognize himself. He had
formed no self-image. He tried to reach through the mirror

to grasp a potato he saw in it; but the potato was being held behind his head. Then, after a few tries and without turning his head, he reached back over his shoulder and grasped the potato. The boy's visual-motor coordination appeared excellent.

Bonnaterre remained skeptical that the boy had spent several winters in the mountains without clothing or fire or proper shelter. He decided to try an experiment.

> One evening, when the thermometer was well below freezing, I undressed him completely, and he seemed delighted to get out of his clothes. Then I made believe I was going to take him outdoors. I led him by the hand down the long corridors to the main door of the Central School. Instead of showing the slightest hesitation about going out, he kept tugging me through the door. From all this, I concluded that the two things are not incompatible. He can both be indifferent to the cold and take pleasure in warming himself by the fire, for one notices that cats and dogs have the same habits.

A few months earlier, this natural scientist and priest had hastened to see the Central Commissioner with an offer to investigate the creature that had turned up in their district. Now, for all his learning and understanding, he did not know what to make of a boy who remained so much an animal yet so resembled a human being. Bonnaterre had to face another possibility that many people must have suggested to him from the very beginning.

> All these little details and many others we could add prove that this child is not totally without intelligence, reflection, and reasoning power. However, we are obliged to say that, in every case not concerned with his natural

needs or satisfying his appetite, one can perceive in him only animal behavior. If he has sensations, they give birth to no idea. He cannot even compare them with one another. One would think that there is no connection between his soul or mind and his body, and that he cannot reflect on anything. As a result, he has no discernment, no real mind, no memory.* This condition of imbecility shows itself in his eyes, which he never keeps on any one object, and in the sounds of his voice, which are inarticulate, and discordant. One can see it even in his gait—always a trot or a gallop—and in his actions, which have no purpose or explanation.

After several months of care, the boy was still more animal than human. Bonnaterre sounds discouraged. He was almost forced into believing that Sicard alone, the miraculous trainer of handicapped children, could bring this creature back to the fold. Out of personal honesty and scientific rigor, he adds: "Provided that the imbecility we have described does not obstruct his training." Only Paris was left.

Life in the Wild

Bonnaterre's observations are invaluable. Without them, we would lack a vital part of the record. If the boy had remained in Rodez, he would have suffered far less trauma than in Paris. I would also have a less interesting story to tell. As it was, both Bonnaterre and the district commissioner wanted to discover as much of the boy's earlier history as possible. Bonnaterre saw an opportunity to publish the first book

---

* These sentences describe the influential eighteenth-century philosophy or psychology of "sensationalism," in which all the contents of the human mind are conceived as arising directly out of sensations (see pages 57–58).

about the Wild Boy of Aveyron. The commissioner apparently realized he was now officially responsible both for a civil case of identity and custody and for a potentially explosive affair watched by scientific and philosophical societies in Paris and elsewhere. The Wild Boy might, after all, be no child of nature at all but a runaway or an abandoned idiot who had wandered for only a few weeks in the woods before turning up in Saint-Sernin.

A different set of circumstances tended to authenticate the case, however. Officials in Saint-Affrique and in Rodez had already identified this boy with a "savage boy" captured briefly six months earlier near another village to the south, really in another mountain range. It took time to hunt out the facts of the case along that mountainous frontier between districts.

The commissioner corresponded with the civil authorities in Saint-Affrique, in Saint-Sernin, and in Albi, capital city of the neighboring Tarn district. He also appointed as investigator an official in Saint-Affrique by the name of Guiraud. Having prepared a preliminary report two days before the boy arrived in Rodez, Guiraud now packed up and headed for the mountains on horseback. He made a good detective. The trail led him seventy miles south, over rugged terrain to the village of Lacaune in the Tarn district. It turned out that several times during the preceding two or three years a boy had been sighted in the area, naked and running wild, feeding on acorns and roots. He had been captured once for certain, possibly twice. People around Lacaune knew the story and had never made very much of it.

Guiraud assembled the following account. Early in 1798, peasants living near a mountain pass south of Lacaune spotted a naked child running through the woods "who fled when anyone approached." Captured and taken to the village, he was put on show in the public square to satisfy the inhabitants' curiosity. He soon escaped and disappeared for over a year. Then in June 1799 three hunters crossed his trail and succeeded in catching him. He was entrusted to a widow, who fed him rye bread and taught him to cook potatoes and other vegetables in the fire. After a week he escaped, presumably in a shirt, whose tatters he still wore when he reached Saint-Sernin. This time a change seems to have come over his behavior and his attitude toward people. Guiraud's official report is explicit about what happened during the boy's last eight months or so living wild in the mountains between Lacaune and Saint-Sernin.

> During the day, he approached farms, walked familiarly into the houses, and waited quietly and without fear to be given something to eat. The pity he aroused and the hospitable customs of the inhabitants of these mountains produced a kindly welcome. Everywhere, people offered him the things he preferred. Then he went away again and hid in the most isolated spots. For a long time he prowled around the mountain of Roquecézière. He repeatedly visited one farm near that village, where he received particularly good treatment. He tossed the potatoes given him into the coals and, before they were fully cooked, pulled them out again and ate them burning hot. Slowly he became familiar with people and his intellectual faculties developed gradually.

Guiraud's account rings true. The evidence indicated, with little room for doubt, that the Wild Boy of Lacaune (Tarn) was also the Wild Boy of Saint-Sernin (Aveyron). Furthermore, one could now estimate that the boy had been living as a "savage" for at least three years, possibly twice that time.

Guiraud apparently found nothing to support stories of the boy having been cared for by a wolf or any other animal.

When taken into custody in Saint-Sernin in January 1800, the boy was neither ferocious nor totally uncivilized. At least during the period after his second capture and escape, he seems to have emerged from a life of complete solitude into a semi-socialized condition. He ceased to fear the sight of other men, and they in turn did not fear him. They helped him and asked for nothing in return except that he not molest them. Though naked, speechless, and filthy, accepting no restraints on his total freedom, he was recognized by the peasants as human. To them he was neither animal nor criminal. The boy in turn seems to have recognized the peasants in their houses as somehow his kind, related to him more closely than the animals. For six months while the autumn of 1799 chilled into winter, the boy and the inhabitants of those distant hills reached an arrangement, a *modus vivendi*, which allowed him to run free among them. He was less domesticated than a dog or a horse, yet unmistakably human. They did not lock him up or insist on clothing him. Most villages had at least one local idiot and took no trouble to hide those cases of flawed humanity. Idiots carried no infection as terrifying to the inhabitants as leprosy or the plague. The boy harmed no one. No one in that sparsely populated countryside took upon himself the responsibility to catch and tame the boy. Thus his "untamed" status achieved temporary social recognition. He had a place in the world.

When the boy crossed the border into the Aveyron district, the surprised citizens of Saint-Sernin had no way of knowing that this creature was anything other than a savage, even a monster, and possibly dangerous. In time, they too might have freed him to roam again. But Saint-Sernin was a more cosmopolitan town than Lacaune, though no bigger, and

Constans-Saint-Estève came bustling out of the commissioner's office aware of his civil and scientific responsibilities.
From that time on, the boy never escaped again for long;
there were only a few brief escapades in Rodez and Paris. He
began to live within civilized society, not on its fringes.

Guiraud notes down a few more details about that brief
period when the peasants around Roquecézière treated the
boy almost like a community mascot. He learned to dig potatoes and other vegetables out of the peasants' fields even when
they were working nearby. They observed him bathing (not
swimming) in streams and marveled at his agility in climbing trees. Thunder and lightning did not frighten him as
they do many animals. But Guiraud devotes a whole paragraph to describing how anxious and uneasy the south wind
made the boy, producing strange body movements and facial
contractions. Guiraud attributes this reaction to severe rheumatism in the boy's right leg; the south wind probably caused
"explosions of pain."

In these stories it is very difficult to tell where the old
wives' tales begin. For example, later evidence about the
boy's fear of heights casts doubt on his phenomenal tree-
climbing ability. Yet the whole set of circumstances taken
together implies something further about the boy that should
not be overlooked. Before this period, and above all before he
was caught the second time and taken to Lacaune for a week,
he must have been much wilder, a real savage unwilling to
let another man approach, self-sufficient, possibly ferocious.
Only during captivity did he learn that men would not hurt
him and would even feed him, and that food could be made
tenderer by cooking. Before those revelations modified his behavior, he must have lived like a frightened animal, scarred
by his fights with other animals, yet without an animal's
instincts to guide him.

Guiraud did not succeed in following the Wild Boy's trail

further back into the past. He located no records, no witnesses, no parents, no nurse. For at least the first four or five years, the boy must have been raised in some kind of environment—even if only a cage or a dark room. But this part of the story remains cloaked in mystery. No one claimed him; no one could identify him before Lacaune. Of course, Guiraud and Bonnaterre and everyone else who investigated the case encountered a rich store of rumor and local folklore. Most accounts are based on some form of cruelty or outright crime. Bonnaterre was prepared to believe one story, but couldn't supply details because it concerned living people:

> According to some very recent information given me by people in whom I have confidence, and according to stories passed around in the canton of ———, this boy is the child of a certain D—— N—— from M——. They say he was born of a legitimate marriage, but the inhuman parents abandoned him after about six years because he did not have the gift of speech.

Several years later, Bonnaterre's text was reprinted in Rodez along with some other documents and a full-length play by a certain Vaisse-de-Villiers. Based on a similar story of inhumanity, the play depicts a jealous husband hiring another man to get rid of his unwanted child. Instead of killing the boy, the man abandons him in the woods and then, driven by conscience, hurls himself off the steep face of Roquecézière mountain to a violent death. (Bonnaterre, having died two years earlier, had nothing to do with the coupling of his sober report with this fanciful horror story.)

In the end, we must accept the boy as he appeared in Lacaune and, later, Saint-Sernin—a rough beast whose story of woe and happiness was only beginning.

Paris

By June 1800, Sicard and the Society of Observers of Man in Paris were becoming impatient. For five months Bonnaterre, backed by the Central Commissioner, had kept his charge five hundred miles away in Rodez. Yet the Wild Boy of Aveyron had become an object of intense interest for the "moral sciences"—we would say the social sciences. When a directive came from the Minister of the Interior conveying 740 francs to Bonnaterre to escort the boy to the capital, there was no way or reason to delay longer.

In mid-July 1800, Bonnaterre and Clair packed up for the trip and did what they could to outfit the Wild Boy for the capital. By this time Clair had grown genuinely fond of the boy. Nothing suggests that he gave them any particular trouble, even though he had escaped and had been recaptured four or five times. In those days, the trip from Rodez to Paris took about a week in a stagecoach that stopped at inns along the way for relief and refreshment. One wonders how the other passengers reacted to this party of three, including a weirdly garbed boy kept on a leash. Bonnaterre and Clair had prepared a special haversack in which to carry his favorite foods. They knew that the inns would not always have those items. The boy quickly noticed what the haversack was for and insisted on having it on the seat beside him when he was in the coach.

> When we arrived at an inn, he waited outside the door and wouldn't go in until the object of his fondest affections had been carried in ahead of him.

On the way to Paris, the boy fell sick with smallpox, a common disease in pre-vaccine days. It was not a severe case. They were delayed ten days, probably in Moulins, and arrived in Paris after eighteen days on the road. The boy still carried fresh scars of the "pox" on his face. Bonnaterre probably worked on his *Historical Notice on the Wild Boy of Aveyron*, a copy of which had already reached the Minister of the Interior.

Everyone had anticipated that the scenery on the trip would make an impression on the boy. Nothing of the sort happened. He paid attention only to his own comfort and regular nourishment, and barely looked out the window. When at last, on August 6, 1800, the stagecoach drove into Paris, he didn't even seem to see the swarming streets and magnificent buildings that dazzled most country folk. Bonnaterre went directly to the Institute for Deaf-Mutes to find Sicard and deliver the boy into his hands. An anonymous article in the *Gazette de France* two days later reported that the Wild Boy was now wearing clothes and had been trained to shake hands. Yet the same article states: "He has not made a single step toward civilization." The boy probably shook hands more like a dog than a human being. In any case, according to the *Gazette*, "the Father of the deaf-mutes" welcomed the Savage into his "interesting family." That was an optimistic version of the boy's arrival. Sicard himself probably wrote the article. (See Appendix I.*)

* The article that followed this one in the *Gazette* reported on a public meeting of the Society of Observers of Man on the day of the Wild Boy's arrival. At the meeting the Society announced a 600-franc prize to be awarded for research in a field described as follows: "To determine, by the observation of one or several babies, the order in which the various physical, intellectual, and social [*morales*] faculties develop, and the degree to which that development is favored or impeded both by the influence of objects in the infant's surroundings and by the even greater influence of the persons who communicate with him." These few lines anticipate not only the later fortunes of the Wild Boy but also the work in developmental psychology of modern figures like Piaget and Anna Freud.

The Institute for Deaf-Mutes occupied several acres of high ground just across the boulevard from the Luxembourg Gardens. Among other things, the institute was famous for an enormous elm tree well over a hundred feet tall that grew in its central courtyard. Visible from all over Paris and said to have been planted by the royal financier Sully in 1600, the elm was called the "Plume of St. Geneviève's Hill." This section of Paris south of the Sorbonne and the Latin Quarter was semi-rural in 1800. Chickens cackled and cows lowed behind high walls. Even today, inside the institute grounds it is almost country—trees, flowers, vegetable gardens, outlying cottages, and a pond. The revolutionary government had turned the former Catholic seminary over to Sicard, and for ten years deaf-mutes of both sexes had lived and gone to school in the five-story stone buildings. A few years after the Wild Boy's arrival, only boys were accepted; the girls were sent elsewhere. The place had a very special atmosphere, almost eerie to a stranger. In class, at meals, playing in the yard, in the dormitories, the students spoke with their hands and bodies. They listened with their eyes, and sometimes made odd noises. Some were very bright; some were devils. The inmates of the institute were if anything more animated than ordinary youngsters.

In spite of his official welcome, the boy was virtually abandoned in the institute. Sicard was busy with students, with administering a large organization, and with writing the first books about sign language. Two weeks after the Wild Boy's arrival, Sicard and Bonnaterre took him for an official visit to the Minister of the Interior, who observed him for half an hour. The boy was described in an unreliable newspaper account as having been overjoyed by the minister's magnificent suite of offices. Bonnaterre stayed in Paris only long enough to have his book printed and distributed. Then he and Clair

went back to Rodez. On leaving, Clair offered to take care of
the boy if he ever needed a home. We would have slight
knowledge of what happened to the boy now if someone else
had not turned up to keep the records. The philosopher and
anthropologist J. J. Virey had just finished an ambitious
book, *Natural History of the Human Species*, with detailed
discussions of monkeys, Eskimos, Hottentots, Indians, and
other "savages." He decided to add a section on the Wild Boy
of Aveyron and visited him many times soon after his arrival.
He also interviewed Clair. In the rest of his book Virey repeated many preposterous stories about creatures he had
never seen. But about the Wild Boy he wrote as a reliable
and intelligent observer and extended Bonnaterre's account
in several directions.

The boy had grown quite fat now, loved to be tickled,
laughed easily, and apparently dreamed while asleep. The
spasmodic movements Bonnaterre mentions seem to have disappeared. Like a domestic animal, the boy was housebroken
to perform his natural functions outside—but still without
modesty. Virey cannot hide his disappointment on two counts.
First, "I am sorry to see the natural man so egotistical." Unable to escape, the boy was concerned only to satisfy his appetite for food. "One would think that his whole being was
focused in his stomach; it is the center of his life." Second,
apart from gluttonous eating, the boy behaved with unre-
lieved apathy. His mind seemed utterly blank, indifferent to
everything and everyone around him. A ceremonial visit by
the Emperor himself in his most magnificent costume
wouldn't have stirred any reaction in the boy. Nothing caught
his attention for more than a few seconds. He occasionally
sucked straws for amusement or reached for a shiny object.
He avoided boys and girls of his own age. "Except for his
human face, what would distinguish him from a monkey?"

Yet Virey insists time after time on the boy's lack of naughtiness or nastiness. He is the perfect innocent, incapable of wishing harm to anyone. The word Virey finds in French for this strange human being is *doux*—mild, sweet, harmless, of good disposition. He applies it to the boy as one would to a perfect pet for children. "I have noticed no clear sign of idiocy in this boy." Virey places great faith in what Sicard will do in training the boy. His closing paragraph, though pompous in style, shows real feelings of pity and hope.

> Go your way, unfortunate young man, through this grievous world, and dissolve your untutored simplicity in the bonds of social existence . . . The path of your education will be sprinkled with tears . . . May you live happily among your countrymen! May you, simple creature, display the sublime virtues of a generous soul and transmit to future generations this honorable example, as the eternal proof of what a child of innocent Nature can do.

Through Virey's account we know the boy's condition and circumstances up to the beginning of September. Then we lose track, and the fragments of information that survive seem to conflict. One writer complains how difficult it is to estimate the boy's mental development because "the boy lives under constant constraints, always tempted to escape, and so restricted that he is led around on a leash attached to his waist." Elsewhere, one receives the impression that he could roam the buildings and grounds fairly freely. Yet it is hard to believe that he wouldn't have found ways to climb over the walls and escape. All the evidence suggests that his condition deteriorated so seriously in September and October that he nearly returned to the "wild" state. Apparently he began soiling his bed. The sweetness Virey had noticed gave way to nastiness.

After the scientific observers like Virey had paid their visits, the curiosity seekers turned out to see this celebrated freak of nature. Many of them managed to get into the institute, probably by greasing the palm of an attendant or using influence. They may have expected an edifying spectacle; what they saw was a disgusting animal. His convulsive movements began again. He bit and scratched his attendants. The doctor at the institute described him in very bad shape.

> Annoyed and victimized during his first three months in the institute by idle curiosity hunters of Paris, and by the so-called observers, who bothered him just as much; wandering around the unheated corridors and the garden in the harshest months of the year; wallowing in revolting filth; often going hungry . . .

But what about Sicard? The famous educator was supposed to take charge of the Wild Boy of Aveyron in the name of the French nation and the Society of Observers of Man and restore him to humanity and to society. At the end of his short book describing the boy's time in Rodez, Bonnaterre stated directly that everything now depended on this "philosophic instructor." Miracles were expected of Sicard, for some of his deaf-mute pupils had made a reputation by their intelligence and wit in answering written questions before large audiences.

There is no record of why Sicard failed to work with the boy. But it is not hard to surmise. Probably discouraged by the boy's utterly uncivilized behavior and lack of response to his approaches, Sicard must have decided that he could never train this brutish creature. He had better not test his reputation on an obviously impossible case.

So the Wild Boy was left to run wild around the institute, friendless, uncared for, fleeing the prying visitors and the deaf-mute pupils, who probably taunted and teased him to the limit. I find no signs of systematic abuse, only of abysmal neglect. It was a curious fate for a boy who had become the talk of the entire nation less than a year earlier and been acknowledged as an official charge of the state.

Examination and Diagnosis

Something had to be done. In one of its earliest official decisions, the Society of Observers of Man had claimed the Wild Boy of Aveyron for science and humanity. Someone had approached Napoleon's brother to request that the boy be entrusted to Sicard. But when Sicard and his colleagues confronted the specimen they had obtained, it seems they found very little to "observe" except his filthy habits and his lack of response to Sicard's celebrated methods for educating the uneducable. Still, they had a responsibility, official, scientific, and even human. Unless they went back to the authorities and asked that the orders be withdrawn—a humiliating admission of defeat—they would have to find some way to handle the case.

The Society of Observers of Man responded in exactly the way such an organization would respond today. They appointed a committee or commission of five members to study the situation and report back. As the person closest to the case, Sicard had to participate: no one questioned his competence. A young anatomist named Cuvier, barely in his thirties and already launched on a brilliant career, was given a place. Cuvier is remembered both for his work classifying animals and for his unexpected opposition to the theory of continuous evolution in favor of "catastrophism," the theory that explains the fossil record of the earth by a series of great catastrophes. Degérando, a "moral philosopher" or psychologist, and Jauffret, a naturalist, were also appointed to the commission. The most distinguished of all was Pinel, a medical doctor concerned with mental disease. His position as head doctor of Salpétrière, the principal insane asylum of Paris, was more important even than Sicard's. Two years earlier, Pinel had published *Nosology*, a lengthy and systematic analysis of diseases according to their symptoms. Late in 1800 his most influential book appeared, *A Medico-Philosophical Treatise on Insanity*. At fifty-five, Pinel was at the peak of his career, and naturally enough the commission chose him as their spokesman and leader. History books describe Pinel as a founder of psychiatry and a pioneer in clinical medicine.

It is difficult to determine just how this commission of five observers went about its work during the fall of 1800. Surely they all examined the boy in the institute, some of them several times, one would suppose. As a comparative anatomist, Cuvier must have taken all the boy's measurements, but no record has survived. No one ran any systematic tests. We never learn whether the boy was right- or left-handed or ambidextrous. With some care, and apparently in whatever situation the boy happened to be in at the time of their visit, they observed his capacity for sustained attention, how he used his five senses to guide himself, the significance of his gestures, and the sounds he made. Possibly because everyone assumed it would be useless, they apparently did not see if the boy would perform any set tasks to gain a reward or to avoid punishment. They did not find out what specialized skills he might have developed in the woods. No one tried to discover how well he could play or imitate or compete. They mention no flaws or malformations except the scar on his throat. In body, at least, the boy seemed to be all there.

Thus, when Pinel wrote the report for the commission in

November 1800, he wasted no time in coming to what he considered the point: the boy's *mental* condition. He began by saying that the boy had nothing to do with *savages*, neither the unscientific kind discussed by Bonnaterre in proposing to add the Wild Boy of Aveyron to the supposed cases of *homo ferus*, nor the real savages found in distant lands and described by travelers. Pinel managed to slip his final verdict into the first paragraph.

> Several months in the Institute for Deaf-Mutes have brought no apparent progress and no sign of perfectibility. However circumspect one must be in making a prognosis, one can see nothing to suggest a brighter future.

After this, Pinel divides his ten-page report into four parts: the boy's physical condition and behavior; a brief description of several cases of mental damage or retardation observed in the two institutions where Pinel saw patients; a comparison of the Wild Boy's condition to those cases; and conclusions, or "inductions." The very outline of the report suggests its conclusions.

The first part does add some information about how the boy acted under certain circumstances, while repeating much that Bonnaterre and others had described.

> His eyesight is so poorly developed that he doesn't seem to tell the difference between a painted object and the real thing, and puts his hand out the same way to grasp both.

Pinel was so impressed by this fact that he mentions it three times. The second time he adds:

One is struck therefore by a lack of coordination between his eyesight and his sense of touch, and that is a
trait I notice among retarded children who have been
put away.

This statement clearly contradicts Bonnaterre's description of
the boy's behavior in front of a mirror. All the other accounts
insist on the boy's great physical dexterity, at least in handling or pilfering food. Pinel's observations do not always
ring true. Sometimes he seems prejudiced.

When one makes a loud sound, he turns around . . . If
one repeats the same sound, he no longer pays attention.
He is totally insensible to music . . . Is there any reason
not to say that in this area even elephants have an advantage over him? . . .
One could well conclude from the way the boy tests
food that his sense of smell is very delicate and cultivated, if one didn't know that he defecates and urinates
right in his bed. This behavior seems to place him lower
than all animals, both wild and domestic.

In measuring the intelligence of apes, modern psychologists
have relied heavily on the capacity to devise and use tools.
Pinel evaluated the boy's conduct in this light and went on to
discuss the crazy sounds he made that seemed to bear no
resemblance to speech or even thought.

This so-called Savage does not even have the instinct to
get up on a nearby chair in order to reach something,
and hits on that course of action only after having been
shown how. When locked in a room with other people,
he seems to remember that he must turn the key in a
specific direction to open the door. But in the months
that I have observed him he has never succeeded in

giving the proper turn to the key. Defeated by the difficulty of the task, he leads someone to the door to let him out. One would be tempted to attribute to a sudden memory or to a burst of vivid imagination the shrill cries and the peals of immoderate laughter which he lets off from time to time, without any apparent cause, and which light up the expression on his face. But I can affirm that very often one sees such sudden outbursts of hilarity or of delirium in idiotic children and adults confined to our hospitals . . . I have long considered them as passing attacks of insanity . . . and sometimes as the consequence of a total absence of ideas.

In the second part, Pinel described several "idiot" children, including a deaf-mute, an albino, and two epileptics. (Today most of these children would not be classified as idiots or even retarded.) Then he went on to consider the cases of apparently normal children who lost their faculties after an attack of convulsions or after a particularly difficult time in growing their first or second teeth, or because the mother had been frightened during pregnancy. The third part stated that the Wild Boy's behavior resembled those cases of idiocy and insanity.

After all this, there was not much left for Pinel to say in his "inductions" except to repeat his estimate of the boy's idiocy and to criticize Bonnaterre for having become so interested in the case. The possibility of Sicard's training the boy was out of the question. Nothing would help him. He should be put away like the rest. As to the cause of the boy's condition, Pinel set aside epilepsy and proposed that it must be one of the three he had just discussed: convulsions, hard teething, or a mother frightened during pregnancy or childbirth. Unfeeling parents, he speculated, must have reacted to the boy's failure to develop by abandoning him in the woods, perhaps during a period of famine. There he might have wandered "for several years, reduced to purely animal instincts." Though the last sweeping sentence of the report is phrased as a question, Pinel makes it clear that he sees no hope for the boy, not even with "lengthy and methodical instruction."

For some reason Pinel did not present his own report. Jauffret read it to the monthly meeting of the Society of Observers of Man on November 29, 1800. He omitted the conclusions—though Pinel's opinion was clear without them —because other members of the commission would also contribute to the final report. But Pinel's is the only written document we have from the group. Cuvier did not dissent. Sicard had already decided that the boy was an incurable idiot. Only Degérando in later discussions at learned societies seems to have had reservations about Pinel's verdict.

Pinel had organized and written his text in some haste. Had he planned to print it, he would surely have eliminated the repetitions and wandering argument. He also displayed a pronounced irritation toward Bonnaterre, probably because Bonnaterre's book had stirred up wide interest in the boy's future and training. That put Sicard, the Society that had brought him to Paris, and even Pinel himself in an uncomfortable position.

The most remarkable aspect of the text is that Pinel left unexamined the possible "organic" or "functional" causes of the Wild Boy's condition. Modern medicine hesitates to use these terms, but they will help clarify what was "wrong" with the boy. If the origin of his mental behavior was *organic*, that would mean that he suffered from some malformation of the brain or nervous system causing abnormal or idiotic behavior and a failure to develop. Such malformation could be caused either by a flaw in his genetic makeup or by physical damage before or after birth. A gene that triggers the growth of tissue

linking certain segments of the brain might have been missing; or he might have fallen on his head. Organic insanity or
idiocy cannot usually be "cured." Often its exact cause, hidden deep inside the body, cannot be found.

If, on the other hand, the origin of the Wild Boy's condition was *functional*, that would mean that his genetic and
physical equipment was normal and intact at birth, and his
upbringing and experiences had affected his behavior and
responses. A mental shock, a deeply hostile environment, absence of stimulation when most needed by his growing nervous system, atrophy of the mind from lack of use—any of
these circumstances might cause serious psychological and
mental malfunction without producing any detectable physical damage. Similarly, there may be nothing basically
"wrong" with a child who cannot learn to read except the
way his whole life has taught him to shield himself against
such a task. The distinction is close to the traditional one
between heredity and environment.

Except for the scar on his neck, which could have indicated
damage to the vocal cords, the Wild Boy apparently bore no
mark of serious injury or physical deformity. His other scars
were superficial. He looked like an ordinary boy—as did
many of Pinel's craziest patients, we can be sure. In his report
Pinel attributed the boy's wild or idiotic behavior to one of
three possible causes of organic damage, none of which could
be proved then or now. He did not even speculate on two
other, equally significant possibilities: that the boy was a
hereditary idiot; or that he was a "normal" boy whose startling condition could be attributed to his years in the woods
isolated from human society, i.e., that he was functionally
retarded. Comparing exterior symptoms, as Pinel did, led to a
tentative diagnosis which satisfied most of the special commission and the Society, but not everyone. The mental patients

Pinel had treated with some success were those who could talk and could form some relationship, no matter how sick or distorted, to people around them. What could he do with a foul boy who could not say a word and who didn't even seem to realize that other people were anything more than devices to feed him and keep him prisoner? The boy had no human sense of being in the world. He had no sense of himself as a person related to other persons. Pinel classified him as an incurable idiot. The diagnosis is hardly surprising. However, we must be more careful with the facts and theories than Pinel could be in 1800.

Diagnosing the Diagnosis

After acting on its scientific and philanthropic principles in bringing the Wild Boy to Paris, the Society of Observers of Man turned its back on the boy. By diagnosing him as an incurable idiot, Pinel and his colleagues snuffed out any lingering hope of finding a "noble savage." Six months later, as we shall see, they would have had to modify their opinion if asked for it again.

Could a similar group today, with modern tests and increased medical and psychological knowledge, do any better? The answer is that there would probably be several diagnoses, not just one. That is precisely what has happened when psychologists in recent years have gone back over the boy's story and given their opinion on the basis of what the documents reveal.

Bruno Bettelheim has spent most of his life working with children so emotionally damaged or so deprived of love and attention at a critical stage of their development that they retreat entirely into themselves or develop what look to us like utterly bizarre means of coping with the world. They won't respond to others, have terrible difficulties with toilet training, and usually cannot talk. They seem to be frozen into tight patterns of behavior. The psychological term for their condition is *autism*, the inability to see or think beyond oneself—selfism. Often such autistic children are diagnosed as untreatable idiots, as the Wild Boy was.

Yet, by surrounding them with an environment of love and understanding, Bettelheim seems to have cured some of the incurables. He also holds bold theories about how the eeriest behavior of these children is not inhuman or crazy but a fully human defensive response to an impossible situation. In his book *The Empty Fortress* (his image for the mere outward shell of a person, with no character and no communication), he discusses the case of the Wild Boy of Aveyron and comes to the conclusion that he was probably an autistic child, not an idiot as Pinel's committee declared. Bettelheim does not make it clear, however, whether he believes the boy was autistic at a very early age and abandoned for that reason, or developed his autism during his years alone in the wild.*

Louis Gayral, a French psychiatrist, has worked more carefully on the case and examined everything he could find about the boy's first contacts with people in Lacaune, Roquecézière, and Saint-Sernin. Gayral emphasizes the rapidity with which the boy learned certain skills during his first captivity and the ease with which he seemed to respond

* Leo Kanner, the child psychiatrist who identified and named the condition in the 1940's, describes autism in terms that vividly evoke certain aspects of the Wild Boy's condition: "The characteristic features consist of profound withdrawal from contact with people, an obsessive desire for the preservation of sameness, a skillful relation to objects, the retention of an intelligent and pensive physiognomy, and either mutism or the kind of language that does not seem intended to serve the purpose of interpersonal communication."

to other human beings. He was not withdrawn, frozen deep into himself, incapable of adjusting his actions to those of others. Gayral therefore rejects Bettelheim's diagnosis of autism. He believes that the lack of social and mental stimulus for five or six crucial years is enough to explain the boy's retarded condition. An autistic child, Gayral implies, like an idiot, would probably not have survived.

O. Mannoni, another French psychologist, does not really attempt a diagnosis but shakes his finger at everyone else who has. He feels the Wild Boy gave signs of much more "intelligence" than he is given credit for, including his strange, liquid "lli" noises (see pages 95–96). And Mannoni proposes that Sicard and Pinel and everyone else would have changed their opinion of the boy's mental capacities if they had taken him out into the woods and tried to live there for a while with him. That way they could have found out what he really knew. In saying this, however, Mannoni chooses to ignore the differences between animal and human intelligence. Obviously, it took some form of semi-instinctual intelligence for the boy to survive as he did. But was he more than an animal? Could he reflect in any way on his own life? Could he form ideas and distinguish past from future? All this modern second-guessing of Pinel's unconvincing report does not carry us very far. Even today a panel of distinguished medical and psychological experts, using electroencephalograms and motor and intelligence tests, would be hard put to decide whether the boy's condition was due to identifiable organic deficiency or to the environment of his formative years.

Harlan Lane, an American psychologist and linguist, has published a book-length scholarly account of the Wild Boy and of Itard's work with him. Lane comes to the conclusion that symptoms of mutism and general retardation were "the result of his isolation in the wild." In other words, the kind of behavior the boy had successfully developed in order to survive in the woods was precisely the behavior that struck "normal" people like Sicard and Pinel as deviant or idiotic.

Thierry Gineste, a young French psychiatrist who wrote his thesis on the Wild Boy and Itard, has discovered many new documents on the case and has filled in much of the historical background. Gineste argues persuasively that we simply do not know enough even now to attempt a reliable diagnosis of the boy's condition. There are many more important aspects of the case to think about, such as why the Wild Boy responded so well to training for a limited period and how the world looked to him from inside his mind.

Gineste's attitude is the soundest of those mentioned. Yet I cannot help nursing an unprovable belief that the Wild Boy was not organically damaged but functionally retarded by years of deprivation. During that time he trained himself in effect to be an animal. If this is the case, then what happened to the boy during the next six years becomes even more significant than the time in the forest. For we believe that functional damage can be at least partially repaired, that what one environment has brought about, a new environment can modify. Just how far the boy would now change back from an animal into a human person provides the best evidence we have about his original condition.

2

The Talk of Europe

The Forbidden Experiment: Human Nature

What I call the forbidden experiment is one that would reveal to us what "human nature" really is beneath the overlays of society and culture. Or at least an experiment that could tell us if there is any such thing as human nature apart from culture and individual heredity.

We argue about these questions more vehemently today than people did a thousand years ago when it was widely agreed that humankind had been created in God's image and had "fallen" into a state of Original Sin. We, too, need to have some notion of how people are basically constituted in order to bring up our own children and deal with strangers and with ourselves. If we believe people are basically selfish,

41

untrustworthy, and aggressive, then we should favor a fairly strict set of constraints and laws to regulate behavior and protect us from one another. If we believe people are peaceful and cooperative under favorable conditions (as the system of democracy assumes), then we should create for every individual as much freedom as possible from outward constraints. But we have been unable to prove or even accept either position. We remain uneasy in our estimate of ourselves.

In the eighteenth century, naturalists and philosophers were preoccupied by the question of human nature because they believed that the whole subject had to be reformulated and answered afresh. Experimental science, political revolution, and "freethinking" philosophy claimed to have overthrown the dogmas of established religion and the class system of hereditary aristocracy. Man began to be seen not as a special being created in the image of God; he was to be redefined in terms of his place in the natural world. In 1735 the great Swedish naturalist, Carl von Linné, published *The System of Nature*, an attempt to classify all living beings, plant and animal, and to regularize the Latin names (including his own, which he changed to Linnaeus). In his vast periodic table based on continuity between species, human beings are far from special. They are tucked away in the class of quadruped mammals, under the order of primates, along with monsters, monkeys, and a new species he called *homo ferus*— wild man. Such an arrangement puts man "in his place" and at the same time implies a whole series of questions. What distinguishes human from animal? Are there missing links making us even closer to animals? What is man's "nature"?

In juggling these questions, the freethinkers of the eighteenth century became particularly interested in three areas: the higher animals close to man (not only apes but also troglodytes, Hottentots, and pygmies, long thought to be animals); lapsed men (like Selkirk and Peter of Hanover; see Appendix II); and man "in the state of nature." This last concept, something like a legal fiction or an algebraic unknown, referred to the hypothetical condition of human beings before they banded together into societies. By a convenient simplification of very diverse thought, it is possible to say that one view pictured "natural man" as a "noble savage" with a peaceful and good disposition; the opposite view pictured him as a nasty brute constantly at war. The former view is usually associated with Jean-Jacques Rousseau; the latter, with Thomas Hobbes. In an age seeking the overthrow of old constraints, Rousseau's optimism was more popular than Hobbes's pessimism.

When the Wild Boy of Aveyron was discovered at the very end of the eighteenth century, it was expected that he would provide scientific observers with a special revelation about human nature. Moreover, he was a home-grown native Savage—neither yellow nor black nor red, just dirty. As a human being who had lapsed back to the animal condition, he should embody man in the state of nature. Serious philosophical articles on precisely this question by Degérando and others appeared in Paris journals within weeks of the boy's arrival.

But the Wild Boy's case raised, even more directly, the question of the forbidden experiment. Theoretically, it has always been possible to perform the forbidden experiment. One needs only to separate an infant very early from its mother and let it develop in nature, with no human contact, no education, no help. Many philosophers have discussed such a project of artificially producing a totally untutored human being. Usually they are concerned to know whether the creature will have the power of speech.* The experiment has allegedly been tried a few times, less out of scientific curiosity than in order to prove a point or defend a cause. The historian Herodotus reports that in the seventh century B.C. the Egyptian pharaoh Psamtik isolated two infants in a mountain hut to be cared for by a servant. Since the purpose of the experiment was to find out what language men speak "naturally," without education, the servant was instructed on pain of death not to talk to his charges. The first reported utterance was the Phrygian word for bread. We are not told what language the servant spoke—or refrained from speaking. The Holy Roman Emperor Frederick II repeated the experiment, also in hopes of discovering man's "natural language." The children died before producing any recognizable speech. Then, in the early sixteenth century, King James IV of Scotland, wanting to demonstrate the ancient origins of his country, is said to have staged the experiment a third time. As predicted—and presumably as arranged—the Scottish children began to speak "very good Hebrew." The misplaced scientism that lurks behind those clumsy "experiments" recurs in a different form among modern psychologists who decide to bring up their children under close observation in specially designed environments—sometimes with apes of the same age—in order to produce reliable data about human beings in general.

Before Montaigne's day, the act of isolating two infants in a hut would not have troubled many people. Worse things happened all the time, including killing or abandoning un-

---

* Montaigne wrote the most concise text three hundred years ago. "I believe that a child brought up in complete solitude, far from all intercourse (which would be a difficult experiment to carry out), would have some kind of speech to express his ideas, for it is not likely that nature would deprive us of this resource when she has given it to many other animals . . . But it is yet to be found out what language the child would speak; and what has been conjectured about it has no great probability."—*Essays*, II, 12

wanted offspring. All over the world the ruling classes considered large segments of the population as not fully human. Slaves, servants, peasants, and women were a form of property which one could dispose of almost as one wished. It required a Papal Bull in 1537 to convince many colonists that the American "savages" were really human—and therefore worth converting to Christianity. Christ's teachings had not modified the ways of man very profoundly.

By the beginning of the nineteenth century, however, a change had come over Europe. The anonymous newspaper article describing the Wild Boy's arrival in Paris refers specifically to the experiment of isolating a child as "desired" by some philosophers; yet the author clearly implies that it is forbidden for humanitarian reasons. (See Appendix I.) Two centuries of "enlightenment" had extended the sanctity of human life to all individuals and had added to it—as our Declaration of Independence and Constitution attest—the concept of individual rights. A person's life was his own property, not to be taken or exploited by someone else even for scientific reasons. A mature person may incur great risks to himself as long as he does not endanger others in the process. But we cannot deprive anyone, particularly an immature child, of his birthright, which includes a minimum of socialization and education. Eric Lenneberg, one of the most intelligent experts on language development in our era, confronts that prohibition with sharp impatience. "The study of the biological basis of behavior in man is severely handicapped by the impossibility of doing crucial experiments that systematically interfere with physiology, growth of structure, and development." The impediments we have erected around certain kinds of investigation (nuclear, genetic, medical) suggest that the idea of forbidden knowledge is not one we have finished with.

In the face of these slowly acquired taboos that blocked

growing scientific aspirations to knowledge, the Wild Boy's return to society was seen as a natural experiment that could be substituted for the forbidden experiment. I think we can now measure the bafflement and disappointment in Virey's description of the boy a few weeks later.

> He seeks no harm, for he doesn't know what that means . . . He just sits there like the true innocent . . . Therefore, it is not possible to affirm that our Boy from Aveyron is either good or bad; he is just mild . . . and has no relation to us at all.

In other words, the boy did not resolve the debate about man in the state of nature. He looked like a dud, and the moral sciences would have lost interest in the case if a new person had not now entered the story and changed its direction.

A Place and a Time

In order to place and to make sense of these events and what follows, one should know something about the kind of world the Wild Boy walked into, about the region that nurtured him and the deep rumblings of history all around him as he grew up. If he had appeared a hundred years earlier, or ten years earlier, or even ten *weeks* earlier, everything would have happened differently; we would probably never have heard of him. As it turned out, the world seemed to be waiting for the Wild Boy—and then scarcely knew what to do with him.

The little village of Saint-Sernin is perched on a hillside in Aveyron, a district of France named after the Aveyron River. Eighty miles north of the Spanish border, it lies closer to the

Mediterranean than to the Atlantic. In summer the fields turn gold with ripe wheat, and sheep graze on the steeper slopes. To the northeast lie the deep splendid gorges of the Tarn River and the village of Roquefort, whose succulent blue-veined cheese was already famous in Rome under the Caesars. Recently, in the limestone caves of Lascaux to the northwest, local residents discovered some of the oldest and best-preserved prehistoric paintings in the world. The colors of the bison and deer and horses have remained so vivid that many archaeologists at first thought they must be forgeries. The Romans settled the busy river town of Toulouse, a hundred miles to the southwest. Set in the midst of this ancient landscape, Saint-Sernin in 1800 was a quiet village of a few hundred peasants and tradesmen, with stone houses, an ancient church, and a flour mill turned by the river below. The landscape and the village are much the same today. But away from the cleared and cultivated valleys, the mountains remained very wild, with only woodsmen's trails and no roads. Hunters often found wolves, wild boar, a few bears, and many smaller animals. The dense forests were mostly hardwoods, including oak, with their crop of acorns, and some chestnuts. Though situated to the south, this region has a fairly rigorous climate—especially at higher altitudes—hot summers and raw winters generally below freezing at night, with moderate snow. The Wild Boy survived severe conditions.

In the late Middle Ages this beautiful region developed a culture of its own and was called Languedoc after the rhythmic language spoken there. Something approaching an aristocratic democracy grew up in the twelfth century, a way of life that tended toward an easy fraternization among classes, tolerance for alien religious beliefs, the abandonment of war as a way of life for the nobles, and the cultivation of the arts, particularly poetry and music combined in the form of song. The troubadours, poets who sang love songs to their ideal and often unseen ladies, influenced the lyric spirit of many parts of Europe. The kings themselves became poets. For a time Dante, the great Italian poet, planned to write *The Divine Comedy* in the language of Languedoc, or Provençal, as it is also called. This corner of history has a flavor all its own.

In this environment a heretical Christian sect took root. Its doctrines came in part from Eastern sources; in part, they embodied a resistance to the temporal power and widespread corruption of the Catholic Church. The Cathars (sometimes called Albigensians, after the town of Albi) believed not that the universe was created by a benevolent and omnipotent God but that a force of evil had created the material world, including human bodies. The faith of the most dedicated Cathars led them to renounce the evils of the physical world and the pleasures of the body. They preached vigorously and made converts until their faith was beginning to supplant the Church of Rome on all levels of society in that region and to endanger the Pope's authority.

In 1208, Pope Innocent III in Rome proclaimed the only crusade in history against a heresy that had sprung up *inside* Christendom. For political as well as religious reasons, the powerful nobles of northern France converged on Languedoc. In a series of bloody conflicts that lasted forty years, they exterminated the Albigensian heresy. That gentle culture disappeared and Languedoc became part of France. It is easy to idealize this medieval interlude of troubadours and heretics and democratic nobles. If the Wild Boy learned to speak in his earliest years before being abandoned, he probably learned a dialect closer to Languedoc than to French.

In 1800, the Middle Ages still lurked in the landscape

around Saint-Sernin, yet recent events affected the Wild Boy more directly. The day he came out of the woods in early January 1800, as if for the opening of a new century, France was holding its breath. For he had walked into an amazing lull in time. That sudden calm in European history, before the wind began to blow again from another direction, helps explain why he received immediate attention and why he was not allowed to disappear back into the Aveyron countryside.

There had been a revolution; the Wild Boy was born just as it began. For a decade, until just three weeks before the Wild Boy's capture, France had been at war with herself and with most of Europe as well. That was long enough for the French to guillotine their bedraggled king after much breast-beating, free themselves from the grip of the Catholic Church, survive the Reign of Terror, and give themselves a whole new calendar with a ten-day week—in order to produce more work.

By 1799 (the year VIII, according to the new calendar), the country was close to exhaustion. Some kind of an end seemed near. Then, during the last three months of the eighteenth century, the political scene changed rapidly. A dazzlingly successful General of the Armies, barely thirty years old, returned to Paris and took over the government without bloodshed. Napoleon Bonaparte had ambition, nerve, and a quick clear mind. After his *coup d'état* on the 18th of Brumaire ("month of mists"), he issued a proclamation.

> Frenchmen!
> A Constitution is herewith presented to you. It ends the uncertainties which the provisional government introduced . . . The Constitution is founded on the true principles of representative government, and on the sacred rights of property, equality, and liberty. The powers which it institutes will be strong and stable . . .

> Citizens, the Revolution is established on the princi-
> ples upon which it was founded: it is over.

The whole document contained sixteen lines. After ten years of violence, this dashing young hero took less than a page to guarantee peace and a return to normal life. It was not to last very long. But no one knew then that more bloodshed, glory, and humiliation lay ahead in the form of Napoleon's empire. In December 1799, France and most of Europe heaved a sigh of relief. *It is over.* The words seemed authoritative, almost magical. The people of France voted for Napoleon's constitution in an avalanche.

During the ensuing lull, citizens began to look around again. Newspapers and magazines, long suppressed by censorship, resumed regular publication. Seeing that the field was clear, scientists and scholars tried to catch up with one another's work. In December 1799, in the shadow of Napoleon's plebiscite, a group of sixty doctors, naturalists, explorers, zoologists, and philosophers founded the Society of Observers of Man. A few weeks later, stories began to appear in the press about the Wild Boy of Aveyron. Because of the timing, people all over France took notice of him, particularly the Society of Observers of Man. He had come on stage just as the eye of the storm passed over.

The Wild Boy and Napoleon never met. The encounter of the dumb savage without culture with the Emperor of Everything who conquered and reorganized all Europe might have produced an appealing scene. Of course, Napoleon must have heard of the Wild Boy. The official who had to decide whether the state would have anything to do with this puzzling creature was Napoleon's brother Lucien, Minister of the Interior for a short period. The case reached the top levels of government almost as rapidly as a military emergency. Then for ten years they had difficulty deciding how to handle it.

By What Right?

When adults hear about the case of the Wild Child, they usually ask how he turned out. They want to know what happened to him and if he grew up to live some kind of useful and happy life. Children, when told about the boy, ask what he was really like and, above all, how he managed to live in the woods all by himself. Young people close to the boy's age when he was captured want to know both those things. But they often ask another, more searching question: What right did anyone have to capture him? Considering the terrible condition of homes for abandoned children, *why wasn't he left where he was in the woods?*

A practical, historical answer must refer to the scientific interest educated persons developed during the seventeenth and eighteenth centuries in the varieties and behaviors of the human species. The Society of Observers of Man stood for this scientific curiosity and "the right to know" about all phenomena, above all about ourselves. Constans-Saint-Estève, the commissioner in Saint-Sernin, had been exposed to this attitude in Paris. He understood that the Wild Boy promised further knowledge. Therefore, the boy became a scientific case history with surprising speed.

But the question about leaving the boy in the woods is really moral—*moral* in the root sense (like *mores*) that concerns conventions of behavior in a given society, and *moral* in the modern sense, invoking principles of right and wrong. The question could easily catapult us into a vast philosophical discussion about the goals of life, the nature of man, natural rights, and the relation between an individual human being and the society that nurtured him. I shall try to keep things simple.

When first glimpsed near Lacaune, the Wild Boy was loping through the woods and fled from human beings. He was unkempt, naked, totally isolated from all human society, unresponsive to any communication. Scars covered his body. He lacked fire, tools, weapons, and what we consider "adequate" shelter. Yet every account agrees that he had survived several winters, as many as five or six, of this crude existence. He had adapted to his surroundings, even though he had in all probability been left in the woods to die, or had been given up for dead after getting lost. Furthermore, the boy was reasonably healthy, though undernourished. By living on plants and roots and perhaps small animals, he had become self-sufficient. He was harmless. No one reports that he raided farms or attacked children. He did not terrify the countryside. From many material and moral points of view, he must be seen as better off and better behaved than, say, a child living in the lower depths of a big European city of that era. A really destitute and neglected slum child, in 1800 or today, is no better nourished than the Wild Boy, may well carry disease, and is probably corrupted by vice, crime, and squalor.

Did the boy have emotions? Was he happy alone in the woods? How can we know? Do we even know about animals: dogs or horses or birds? He made strange noises and laughed after a fashion. On his terms, whatever they were, he seemed to be satisfied with his lot. He kept to himself and did not want more than to feed his hunger and sleep when he was tired. Anything beyond that had to be thrust upon him.

We have learned slowly and painfully that we must be careful of the consequences when we tamper with the environment, when we upset an existing balance of nature. By lying low and barely moving, the Wild Boy had found a balance—a very limited one. Just what right, or duty, did anyone have to remove this boy from the life he had made for himself? He had passed the first fundamental test: survival. For years, no one had helped him. His situation seemed to call for the most basic response: live and let live. Doesn't any other response, any wish to change the boy's life, reveal the worst in us—presumptuousness, arrogance, idle curiosity, cruelty?

Nothing I can add will remove or diminish the urgency of such questions. They are very real. The strength behind them helps explain why the oldest stories, from Egyptian myths and Aesop's fables to Walt Disney, are about animals. Every generation has had its Tarzan and has become excited about stories of wolf children. We yearn for a new Eden. Our cares are heavy. Still, we must look longer at these matters.

There have been and there are still societies in which parents expose their infants in order to test their sturdiness. And here precisely lies the difference. If they survive, those children are not left alone to live in the wild. They are taken back into society and "brought up," usually by their parents, to take a full and responsible place in the community. If the Wild Boy's parents had ever come forward or been identified, they might have been punished for negligence. Yet it would have been considered both their right and their duty to claim him, and to raise him up out of his animal-like condition. In their absence, however, society itself tends to claim such a child, to care for him and to expect him to do his part in the communal life. Constans-Saint-Estève never gave any explanation of his conduct, yet something prompted him to make the decision he did. He perceived well enough that the boy had survived and might well go on living in his wild state. He also perceived that the boy had been deprived of what every parent gives its offspring: the benefits of social exchange and a place in a collective life.

Constans, like all of us, acted on the basis of strong undeclared assumptions. Without even thinking about it, he believed that the experiences and rewards of social life exceed those of mere survival as an animal. The peasants around Roquecézière were willing to tolerate what Constans put a stop to—a clear departure from the social order. As Constans saw the situation, total isolation had dispossessed the boy of his birthright as a human being.

What would the rest of us do if, for example, we found an apparently "savage" boy pinned alive under a fallen tree in the remote woods? It's an unlikely but not impossible event. Imagine that such a boy has only one response: to escape. The easiest solution would be to free him. Yet we might well think twice. When he reaches full size, will this creature become dangerous to other people? Don't all of us have a duty in such circumstances to help our fellows to become fully developed human beings? That may be a rash presumption. It may also reflect a slowly acquired attitude of respect and love for others. We condemn people who live by materialistic values alone, whose selfishness knows no bounds but the satisfaction of their appetites. Man has higher capacities. Wasn't selfishness the Wild Boy's condition, because no one was there to help him or for him to help? Every human being has a parent or foster parent until at least the age of five or six, and usually until puberty. If parents do not rear a child to find his way in society, we assume that they have failed him or that something went wrong. Should that damage be left unrepaired by society? There need be nothing false or proud about the usual response: help the child.

These questions should make us understand how difficult it would have been simply to let the boy run wild. And I believe that, once he was captured, it would have been wrong. In his case, there are also special aspects that cannot be ignored.

By the time he reached Saint-Sernin and snooped around the tanner's garden, the boy's adjustment to society had already begun. The two occasions when he was caught and held in Lacaune without undue mistreatment had started the process. He had changed his ways and his attitudes even more during the six months he subsisted near Roquecézière on handouts from the peasants. Of his own accord, he seems to have wandered very close to human habitations, and to have tolerated human beings. There is no indication that he violently resisted capture in Saint-Sernin; he just wanted to run off to the woods at any opportunity. A few weeks later, Bonnaterre and Clair did not find him particularly hard to handle.

Once he was taken and his case reported, it was clearly unthinkable that the boy should be abandoned again. Instead, his very presence and his animal-like habits became a challenge to prevailing ideas of humanity and to the society that had originally pushed him out. He was a total stranger, an alien among men. Yet religion, civil law, and the concerns of scientific knowledge all made it impossible to give the boy back to nature. Once his education was begun, it was necessary to go on until he ceased to respond and improve. Thus, his fate was set almost from the start, when he was first taken captive. It is only from a distance, two hundred years away, and by bringing in perplexing ideas about happiness, free choice, and the balance of the environment, that we can question what happened. Do we have good reasons to denounce the motives of the tanner, Constans-Saint-Estève, Bonnaterre, and others, in making the Wild Boy a prisoner of culture and society? My answer is no. For we are all that kind of prisoner from birth; some part of us knows that in order to be human we need the restrictions we dream of throwing off.

Wisdom in the Eighteenth Century

The peasants around Roquecézière came to terms fairly easily with the boy's wildness. He didn't upset them or challenge their way of life. Even Bonnaterre took the boy pretty well in stride by finding a classification for him, *homo ferus*. We are disturbed by what we cannot recognize and give a name to. But in Paris the boy dropped into the middle of several heated quarrels about the origin and nature of man. In 1800, when the Wild Boy appeared, philosophy had been very active in England and Europe for a hundred fifty years. Furthermore, philosophy still included most of the areas we now call natural science, political science, and social science.

The great contest of philosophy that concerns us in thinking about the Wild Boy began in the seventeenth century with a Frenchman by the name of Descartes. He proclaimed that he rejected all previous authority and relied entirely on his own experience and understanding, reinforced by mathematics. That was a very bold claim, and Descartes was considered a dangerous thinker. One of the bases of Descartes's philosophy was that the mind exists separate from the body (which he represented as a machine) and is not ruled by the body or by the material world around us. Most of us take that point of view when we talk about free choice, or deciding something, or willpower. But an awkward aspect of Descartes's dualism was the split he accepted between mind and body, even though it may correspond to the way we ordinarily think and talk. How do you move from one to the other? He also assumed that our minds are endowed from birth with "innate ideas," universal principles or capacities we do not acquire from experience. Descartes's concept of mind, which his critics have called "the ghost in the machine," would not fit into any simple mechanical model of things like clockwork. In that respect he did not follow the scientific trends of his day. Still, Descartes seemed to get rid of much stuffiness and nonsense. He is rightly known as the founder of modern philosophy.

A half century after Descartes, a down-to-earth Englishman called John Locke formulated a philosophy that moved in a very different direction. He rejected all innate knowledge, along with the notion of the human mind separate from its material body. Our understanding, which "is for the most part passive" and like "white paper" or a "dark room," receives its ideas from sensations and our reflections on those sensations. He did accept the "natural faculties" of understanding and will. Locke never explained satisfactorily how a sensation becomes an idea, for he didn't want to admit anything into the process except matter. There, of course, lay the appeal of his system: he derived everything we know from physical matter, without mind, free will, and innate ideas. His system is called sensationalism or empiricism.

To explain their philosophy, Locke and other eighteenth-century thinkers developed several comparisons that became almost poetic—like light-years or black holes in modern astronomy. Philosophers like to use the Latin expression *tabula rasa*. It means smooth tablet, clean blackboard, blank tape. It stands for the condition of our minds at birth— empty, yet ready to receive or record. Another favorite figure was *man the machine*. Since this was the era when clocks and automatic machines were being perfected, it seemed right to reduce everything in man, anatomy and thought and consciousness itself, to a mechanical model. Condillac, a French priest, went a step further. In order to suggest an inactive mind that merely registers sensations, he borrowed the metaphor of a *statue* gradually brought to life by sense impressions and lacking only language. He too failed to explain how. Above all, he wanted to go beyond Locke in demonstrating that we are born without innate faculties or ideas. Sensory perceptions, Condillac believed, mold both mind and character.

The influence of Locke's empiricism was enormous, especially in France and England. He made everything seem even simpler than in Descartes's dualistic system of mind and body. Mind, for Locke, was a word that referred to matter operating in human beings, going through its natural motions. Since the mind merely receives impressions and does nothing without external stimulus, various forms of determinism invaded philosophy. Many philosophers described men as pure products of their environment. Psychologists are still thinking in these terms today when they speak of "conditioning" as the primary source of our behavior. Most social scientists continue to consider their methods empiricist. Recently, particularly through the work of Noam Chomsky in the field of language acquisition, the theory of innate human capacities shaping our grasp of reality and therefore our behavior has made a strong comeback against the theory of the *tabula rasa*. If our essential bodily organs are already articulated at birth, is it likely that our minds start out empty and formless?

However, Locke's philosophy had another, different consequence. If the physical circumstances of life determine how men live, then by changing those circumstances one can reform men's lives. Nothing could be more logical. (Of course, there's a big hole in the argument. How and why would any person be moved to carry out such changes?) This line of thinking stimulated eighteenth-century politics in its desire to improve men's lot in life. Thus, the doctrine of empiricism that turned some men into determinists inspired others to be reformers and activists. Philosophy is full of such paradoxes.

The reformist line of thinking affected certain categories of people who had been dreadfully treated until then, virtually cast out of the human race. The argument goes like this. If criminals are made and not born, then they can be made whole again, or at least helped. The same reasoning applies to madmen. They should not just be chained up in asylums but treated, given hope. And above all, one set of outcasts, often confused with the insane and locked up with them, deserves special treatment because their handicap is not mental or moral but physical: deaf-mutes. Reform could not heal their physical flaw, but a new environment in which they could use a sign language of their own would restore them to a place in society. This is the subject of the next chapter.

During this period, then, a few devoted individuals driven by current philosophical ideas began to take an interest in social outcasts, and to try to assist them. That is how the famous Frenchman, Tocqueville, came to America in 1830. His mission was to inspect prisons, and that trip inspired a great book about the new democracy. Our modern concern with the mentally ill and the deaf goes back to the eighteenth century. When the Wild Boy turned up, he appeared to be a deaf-mute. That is why the Abbé Sicard was ready to take responsibility for him at first.

Deaf-Mutes and Madmen

The standard version of history records the succession of great rulers, the institutions through which they ruled, and—

at endless length—the exploits of men at war. It makes a grisly tale in which many gifted leaders show a seamy underside of cruelty or megalomania. It is also far from the complete account. Given its full range, history has revealing things to tell us about how different peoples have worshipped or played or eaten over the centuries, how their arts have developed, and how certain ideas like holiness and genius and freedom have come to exert tremendous power. One of the most neglected yet significant stories of all is the way different societies have treated persons who do not fit in, who for various reasons cannot play a full role in the general life.

Until early modern times in Europe, misfits were lumped together, with few discriminations, and confined to institutions known as shelters or hospitals. The obviously sick were supposed to be cared for separately, but were sometimes thrown in with the other unfortunates. Thus the poor, the unemployed, the debtors, the handicapped, the insane, the retarded, the alcoholics, and many criminals were locked up together in vast buildings like the Bicêtre in Paris, which had formerly been used to segregate lepers. (The terrible scourge of leprosy had died out about 1700, for unknown reasons.) The most violent cases—usually the insane—were chained up. Conditions were unspeakable, scandalous enough to cause an occasional royal commission to investigate the health hazard to other citizens in the area. These institutions were left in the hands of the police. The inmates, considered subhuman, received little charity and no treatment.

Among them were the *dumb*. In many languages there is a corresponding word meaning both incapable of speech (probably because of deafness) and stupid. By an ancient association built into the language itself, we consider anyone deprived of speech as stupid and inferior: dumb. The French *sourd* (deaf) has the same connotations. In the early eighteenth century the deaf-and-dumb, unless cared for by family or friends and given some social training through gestures, ended up with the other outcasts in miserable confinement.

Around 1750, something different began happening in Paris. A Spanish priest by the name of Pereire, who had been in love with a deaf-mute girl in his youth, opened a school to educate deaf-mutes. Periere taught them lip reading and the movements of vocal speech. Much of his training was based on touch—touching the throat and lips, actually putting the fingers inside the mouth in order to teach or learn the proper positions. (Helen Keller learned by many of these methods.) A few years after Periere, a French priest called the Abbé de l'Epée opened a school in which he taught not vocal speech but sign language. After a few years he began staging public performances at which he dictated in signs to his students, who wrote in French, Latin, Italian, and Spanish. Hundreds of people from all over Europe came to watch, admire, and learn. Just before the Revolution, the city of Paris and the king himself began to help l'Epée in his good works. He died just a year before the school was made into a National Institute in 1790 by the revolutionary government.

By this time Sicard had been appointed director and began to improve l'Epée's system of sign language. Sicard made his reputation through his prize student, Massieu, who not only could take dictation but could actually express his own thoughts in written French. During the early stages of the Revolution, Sicard was thrown into prison and several times came within inches, or seconds, of losing his life to the blood-thirsty mob. Massieu courageously drew up petitions and intervened in favor of his master by insisting that Sicard was desperately needed as "father" to the deaf-mutes at the institute. Saved in part by his own pupil, Sicard went into hiding and occupied his time by writing an important book about how he trained Massieu in sign language. *Course of Instruction for a Deaf-Mute* was published in 1800, just when the case of the Wild Boy was being talked about.

By a seeming miracle, the dumb could now communicate with each other and even with ordinary people. It became a custom to test their intelligence by asking them questions in public. Massieu and a few other clever deaf-mutes amazed everyone by their precise and often witty answers. What is gratitude? "The heart's memory," responded Massieu. What is the difference between desire and hope? "Desire is a tree in leaf; hope is a tree in bloom; enjoyment is a tree bearing fruit." Thus the dumb could do more than speak; they produced *bons mots*, pithy or poetic sayings that were reported in the newspapers, passed from mouth to mouth, and published in collections. The outcasts became soothsayers and oracles, redeemed by the insight and patience of men like Periere and l'Epée and Sicard.

Such good works as these finally reached the inmates of Bicêtre, the very dregs of society. Just when France entered the period of the Terror, the revolutionary government named to the staff of Bicêtre not a police official as before but the distinguished doctor Philippe Pinel, who later wrote the report on the Wild Boy for the Society of Observers of Man. Many unfounded but influential stories have come down to us about the reforms Pinel introduced after surveying the inmates and their dreadful conditions. He is said to have created a scandal by unchaining the madmen. He also began to classify and even to treat the mental cases. Some consider Pinel the first psychiatrist. In the lore of psychiatry and mental therapy, one scene has become legend.

One of the strong-men of the Terror was a provincial lawyer named Couthon, who inspired great fear because he was crippled and usually had to be carried in a chair. When he visited the Bicêtre to find out if any political prisoners were hidden there, Pinel led the men carrying Couthon to the wards where the insane had been unchained. The inmates responded to Couthon's questions with curses and crazy speeches, without the slightest respect for his person. Everyone expected retaliation, perhaps against Pinel. As he was carried out, Couthon turned to the doctor. "Well, Citizen, you must be crazy yourself to want to unchain such animals." Pinel was as calm as his charges were excited. "I'm convinced, Citizen," he replied, "that they're unmanageable because they have been deprived of air and freedom for so long." He kept his job, and the madmen were not chained up again.

For the kind of good works performed by l'Epée and Sicard and Pinel, someone in the eighteenth century coined the word *philanthropy*. As philosophy means love of wisdom, philanthropy means love of mankind (*anthropos*). Of course, as long as people believed that most important qualities of character and mind are inherited along with social rank and wealth, there was little rationale for trying to change men's lot. But Locke's doctrine of empiricism not only undermined the hereditary privileges of kings and nobles; it also offered a justification for philanthropy. For one could rescue the scum of humanity—the mad or the wicked or the dumb—by improving the conditions in which they live and learn. Dedicated individuals, and the government itself, began to try to improve the lot of the outcasts of society, less out of Christian charity than out of a philosophical belief about how we develop into what we are.

CHRONOLOGY 1770–1840

The Wild Boy

1770	

1780	
	1788–90?: born in south-central France, probably near Lacaune (Tarn)

1790	
	1795–97?: abandoned or lost in forest near Lacaune
	Spring 1798?: first capture and escape

Closely Related Events	*Other Dates and References*
April 25, 1774: birth of Itard in Oraison (Basses-Alpes)	1774: death of Louis XV; Louis XVI becomes king
1775: Condillac praises the Abbé de l'Epée for his work in training deaf-mutes in sign language	1776: Declaration of Independence of U.S.A.
	1778: death of J.-J. Rousseau
	1780: death of Condillac
	1789: outbreak of French Revolution; Declaration of Rights of Man; Blake's *Songs of Innocence*
1790: Sicard appointed director of newly established Institute for Deaf-Mutes	
1792: Constans-Saint-Estève in Paris to represent Saint-Sernin at the National Convention of the revolutionary government	1792: Republic proclaimed
	1793 Louis XVI guillotined
	1793–94: Reign of Terror
1796: Itard, 22, arrives in Paris to study medicine	
1797: *Victor or the Forest's Child*, melodrama by Pixérécourt	
1798: Pinel's *Nosology*, on medical diagnosis	1798: Coleridge and Wordsworth's *Lyrical Ballads*

June 1799: second capture, held a week in Lacaune

1800

Jan. 9, 1800: capture in Saint-Sernin (Aveyron)
August 1800: taken to Institute for Deaf-Mutes, Paris

1801: Itard's first report on Wild Boy

1806: Itard's second report; end of training

1810

June 1811: boy and Madame Guérin move out of Institute for
Deaf-Mutes to house nearby

1820

early 1828: dies in Paris; no details known

1830

1799: Society of Observers of Man founded	1799: (18 Brumaire VIII) Napoleon becomes First Consul by *coup d'état*

	1801: Chateaubriand's *Atala,* novel about a "noble savage" in America
	1804: Napoleon crowned Emperor by the Pope
	1808: Goethe's *Faust I*
	1809: Napoleon at height of power

	1815: Napoleon defeated at Waterloo; banished to Elba

	1820 and after: French romantic poetry and drama
1821: Itard's *Treatise on Maladies of the Ear and Hearing,* his major medical work	
1828: Itard publishes an article on mutism caused by brain damage; implies he may have been "mistaken" in believing he could train the Wild Boy adequately	1828: Kaspar Hauser appears in Nuremberg

1838: death of Itard	

3

Markings on the Tabula Rasa

(NOVEMBER 1800 TO AUGUST 1801)

A Fresh Start and a Foster Father

After his arrival in Paris in August 1800, the Wild Boy spent three frightful months. The adults responsible for him alternately neglected, annoyed, and petted him. The young inmates in the institute sometimes attacked him; he fled to the farthest corners of the garden or hid in abandoned parts of the building. After five secure months in Rodez, cared for by Clair and Bonnaterre, the boy had no one in Paris to protect him in an unfriendly environment.

Meanwhile, his sponsors, having looked him over, were getting ready to throw him back like an undersize fish. Since they could not just free him again in the woods, they were prepared to put him in a man-made jungle called an insane asylum. What else could they do? The boy had become almost impossible to handle and was surely a disruptive presence in an institution devoted to the care of children needing systematic training to overcome their deafness. When he grew to maturity, the boy might well become dangerous. The experts had generally decided that his case held little significance for the moral sciences. Not only in Pinel's report but in the events of these months of disappointment, one hears the splashing sound of people washing their hands of responsibility for the case. Apparently no one remembered Clair and his offer to take the boy back if there was ever need.

A new element enters the story now. Sometime during the summer or fall of 1800, Sicard needed a doctor at the institute because of an accident. The twenty-five-year-old medical student who answered the call worked as an intern in surgery at the Val-de-Grâce Hospital down the street. Sicard liked the young man and found him competent. They became friends, and the surgeon began coming to the institute both to visit the director and to take care of the students. He also became interested in the problem of treating and training deaf-mutes. This young man's name was Jean-Marc Gaspard Itard.

Itard was apparently not on the scene when Bonnaterre and Clair brought the Wild Boy of Aveyron to the institute. But as time went on he had opportunities to watch the boy and hear about what was going to happen to him. Sicard probably told Itard during the fall that the boy had no business being there and that even the most gifted of teachers could not train an unresponsive imbecile to learn sign language. At some point Itard must have taken an interest in the case; he began to observe the boy closely and perhaps to test his reactions. By the end of November or the beginning of

December, Itard was working regularly with the boy according to some kind of plan and changing his living arrangements. Then, on November 29, 1800, the Society of Observers of Man listened to Pinel's report, which classified the Wild Boy as an incurable idiot, a hopeless case. Itard attended the meeting and noted every point so that he could remember the report. A month later, on December 31, the official announcement was made of Itard's appointment as resident medical officer of the Institute for Deaf-Mutes at a yearly salary of sixty-six francs. The position included an apartment for him in the institute building and probably some understanding about his responsibility for the presumed idiot.

The confusion in this sequence of events is evident. Exactly when everyone else was ready to send the boy away as a dead loss, Itard proposed to keep him at the institute and to develop a special training program for him. How are we to interpret these conflicting facts? Was it arrogance that made the young doctor fly in the face of the most authoritative professional opinion? Was he deeply impregnated with eighteenth-century philanthropy? Did he have any concrete reason to believe that the boy should not be sent to the Bicêtre asylum with the insane and other outcasts? Had he glimpsed some exciting medical or scientific significance in the boy's situation?

Itard's life provides a few clues, and we should know something about this new character in the story. Itard had never been abandoned; he never lived in the woods. Yet it is hard not to see him as a "loner." Born in 1774 in the tiny village of Oraison near the Alps, Itard was sent away to school in Marseilles. His parents expected him to go into banking, but the Revolution and the accompanying wars caught up with the boy when he was nineteen. He would normally have been drafted to fight the English and the Dutch; instead, his father and uncle obtained a post for him in the medical services. Itard worked with a famous surgeon, whom he followed to the Val-de-Grâce Hospital in Paris in 1796. He must have worked hard, for within a short time he won appointment as surgeon second-class by competitive examination. He completed his medical studies in 1803. His later career was very successful, yet he remained a bachelor all his life and generally anti-social. The duties at the Institute for Deaf-Mutes led him into medical research on hearing and the ear. He turned down an important appointment in Russia and accepted a medal instead. In 1821 he became a member of the Academy of Medicine. The unpronounceable medical specialty he founded is still taught and practiced today: otorhinolaryngology, the study and treatment of ear, nose, and throat. He published several books.

Itard's education had given him a little grounding in the classics: he trained with some of the best doctors in Paris. We know from his writings that he had absorbed a few basic ideas of seventeenth- and eighteenth-century philosophy, particularly from Condillac. His career reveals a mind very much alive and by no means content with the routine practice of the medical profession in his day. But outside his professional contacts he seems to have lived very much to himself in his apartment at the institute, and later in the center of Paris, capable of long and exhausting work. His cures had the reputation of practicality, and sometimes eccentricity. He treated a woman who complained of buzzing in her ears after surviving a bad fire by sending her to live for a time near a factory that made a terrible racket. This counter-irritant or distraction is said to have cured her. Dr. Itard's insight was not confined to anatomy and the treatment of the tissues. His writings demonstrate that he understood the difference between organic and functional complaints. Perhaps this is why he volunteered to assume responsibility for the Wild Boy when no one else would have him.

Itard died in his early sixties, having trained many students. He left a thousand francs to establish an annual prize for the best discovery in practical or therapeutic medicine. He left eight times that sum to the deaf-mutes with whom he had worked all his life. The money was to pay for a regular reading class so that the students who learned sign language and lip reading could continue their education in books. Itard's biographers liked to say that he looked like King Henry IV of France—a good and noble king.

This, then, was the man who stood between the Wild Boy and confinement in an asylum. In effect, Itard became his foster father, though apparently no legal papers were signed. But he now held an official position at the institute, where the boy would continue in residence. Itard was only thirteen years older than his charge; he was a whole generation—thirty years—younger than the Observers of Man, the eminent men of science who had originally claimed the boy and then rejected him. Sicard and Pinel, the two principal figures, may have felt a little hesitant about assigning the Wild Boy to an unknown doctor after all the publicity about the case. But they apparently did not put any obstacle in Itard's way. For this willingness to step aside and let someone else carry on an investigation that they themselves believed would be totally fruitless, we should be grateful. The records show that Itard was given a completely free hand with the boy.

Itard's Wager

Itard made his decision about the Wild Boy sometime in November 1800. The twenty-five-year-old medical student bet against the two men in Paris on whom his career depended most closely. Pinel was one of the most honored professionals in France and the chief representative of the branch of medicine which Itard wished to join. Sicard had official responsibility for the Wild Boy and for the institution to which both the boy and Itard had been assigned. Why did Itard step forward like David against two Goliaths? It is worth reflecting further on his motives.

Itard devoted himself to his medical work with few distractions. His only family were the deaf-mutes among whom he lived. In such a person, genuine compassion for the woes of mankind lies very close to a form of ambition. St. Vincent de Paul and Albert Schweitzer combined these drives even more dramatically. Itard's ambition drove him more toward knowledge and independence of thought than toward money and fame. He believed that the lot of man could be improved and wanted to make his contribution. His enterprising mind was able to fit together two important aspects of his experience. First, Itard's frequent visits to the Institute for Deaf-Mutes (before he became a resident early in 1801) allowed him to observe the Wild Boy closely when others had lost interest. Several passages in his later reports suggest that during these visits he saw something—a fleeting look on the boy's face, a spontaneous reaction to a situation, perhaps his peaceful meditations squatting on the edge of the pond—that gave the impression of potential responsiveness and intelligence. Second, Itard had a theory. He had Locke's and Condillac's theory that we are born with empty heads and that our ideas arise from what we perceive and experience. Having experienced almost nothing of society, the boy had remained a savage. What he needed was reeducation—from the very beginning.

Perhaps these factors are enough to explain Itard's wager that he could do something with the boy. But the determining element seems to be missing. I believe that, without ever expressing it, Itard must have had a hunch, an insight that made the final difference and shaped the rest of his career. He sensed that the Wild Boy was not an idiot but a special kind of missing link, a creature in whom one could observe how a human being may fail to develop into a socialized adult because of lack of stimulus. If this "animal" or "infant" could be restored to the human capacities of his age level, then the *tabula rasa* theory of learning would gain persuasive proof. Itard believed that he had stumbled upon the possibility of performing a crucial experiment—in effect, the forbidden experiment.

In a sense, there was a precedent; as a surgeon, Itard must have been familiar with it and he probably read about it in Condillac and Voltaire. In 1728, for the first time, a person blind from birth was restored to sight by an operation. The English surgeon William Cheselden accomplished the feat by removing the cataracts from a young man's eyes. But afterwards the cured patient still could not "see." He registered only a shifting, almost painful blur that had no meaning and conveyed no sense of a real world out there related to the world he could understand by touch. Everything seemed to be scraping his eyeballs. It was a long time before he learned to coordinate his sense perceptions, to distinguish shapes, to judge relative size, to tell parts from wholes, and to perceive space and depth. The Wild Boy was neither blind in his eyes nor deaf in his ears, but he used only a tiny segment of his perceptual apparatus. In learning gradually to perceive what seems evident to the rest of us, he would reveal many things about how ideas and faculties and feelings develop. This process is not easy to observe in children. Itard understood that if special training could restore the boy to his age level, the course of events would be worth watching and recording.

I believe that Itard really expected the boy to come to life like Condillac's statue by the mere impress of sensations on his waiting mind. This man of science dreamed of an empirical miracle. Things turned out to be more difficult than that. But those theories about how we form ideas carried Itard beyond psychology and medicine into mythology. He was not simply a doctor treating a patient whom he imagined sometimes as a statue. He had become Pygmalion, the legendary King of Cyprus who fell in love with the ivory statue he was carving. In answer to his prayers, the gods turned the statue into a beautiful living maiden, whom Pygmalion named Galatea. Itard's scientific and emotional attraction to the Wild Boy must have been powerful. He was drawn to the black sheep, to the stone the builders rejected. Here was a lost soul to be rescued.

After his fashion, Itard the scientist was "in love" with this rude creature, whom he wanted to mold into a man after his own image. If we probe to the center of his project, there is something as touching and as outrageous as Pygmalion's prayer and as Narcissus' desire for his reflection, something as audacious as Prometheus' theft of fire, symbol of creation. For Itard presumed to confer, if not life, at least intelligence and humanity.

Fortunately, Itard's ambitions did not blind him to the fact that he was a busy man and would need help. He understood that the boy would respond well to someone like Clair, who had devoted all his time to establishing some form of human relationship with his charge. Itard had the good sense to choose a woman, of an age to be both maternal and undaunted by the boy's erratic behavior. Madame Guérin lived with her husband at the institute in quarters near the kitchens. Their children, who did not live with them, visited regularly. The husband probably worked on the premises.

Madame Guérin seems to have been around forty. She devoted not just the next five but the next twenty-seven years of her life to the boy, who now had both a foster father and a foster mother.

Madame Guérin had no special training, no theories of education, no career to make, no books to write, no fame to win. She was an "ordinary" person; she must also have been a remarkable human being. Many times Itard comments on the steadiness and effectiveness of her care. If we consider the division of time between them and the importance of the natural attachment that grows up between mother and son, we must assign as much credit for the Wild Boy's development to Madame Guérin as to Itard. The doctor could not possibly have gone on without someone like her. She also reported to him about the boy's behavior—how he slept, his movements and responses, the outings they began to make together to nearby parks and gardens. She was always *there*, physically and emotionally. Madame Guérin's name should be remembered with as much honor as Itard's in the events that follow. He would surely have agreed.

The Wild Boy had his own room on the fifth floor of the institute, apart from the deaf-mute inmates and above the Guérins' apartment. He ate with Monsieur and Madame Guérin, and at times Itard seems to have joined them even though the Guérins were simple people of little education. It is impossible to find out from the documents just how confined the boy was at the beginning and as time went on. References to locks and keys suggest that at least for considerable periods he was locked in his room. Other passages imply that he had a good deal of freedom to roam.

Almost all our information about the next few months comes from a report Itard made the following summer to the Society of Observers of Man. Since he arranged those fifty pages analytically by subject and not chronologically in the order of events, many details become blurred or displaced, or simply never appear. For example, he never tells us how the boy was toilet-trained again. We know from other sources that the boy learned to use a chamber pot in his own room. Itard does not give so clear an idea as Bonnaterre did of the daily schedule of eating and sleeping and the times between. And even though it states the case several times, Itard's report as a whole does not follow the development of a surly suspicious animal into a responsive, near-human personality to whom both Madame Guérin and Itard became devoted. It all happened, as Itard tells us himself, "in the short space of nine months"—November to August. That speed is the best demonstration that Itard's new rearrangement of the boy's life worked effectively as a means of bringing out his latent faculties and feelings.

Everything was done according to a plan based on Condillac and Locke, and on the "moral treatment" advocated by Pinel and by some English Quakers who had opened a home for the insane. Today, instead of moral treatment, we would probably say psychotherapy. The plan had five goals:

1. To give the boy the ability to respond to other people
2. To train his senses
3. To extend his physical and social needs
4. To teach him to speak
5. To teach him to think clearly

Those goals correspond to the five sections of Itard's report. Unfortunately, we do not have the daily notebooks on which he must have based his account. Still, by reading between the lines and adding a few other items of information, it is possible to reconstruct a fairly complete story of how the Wild Boy fared between November 1800 and August 1801.

Sensitivity Training

Itard's first concern was to reach this creature who spent his time "squatting in a corner of the garden" and to "attach him to society." He and Madame Guérin would have to make it possible for the boy to live with other people, to emerge from the solitary existence in which he merely satisfied a few biological necessities. Itard hoped to reach the boy first by making his life agreeable.

> We had to make him contented on his own terms, by letting him go to bed at dark, furnishing him an abundance of food to his liking, letting him do nothing if he wanted, and taking him out on walks in the open air. They were more like runs, no matter what the weather. These expeditions out to the fields seemed to please him even more when there was a sudden and violent change in weather. It would seem that no matter what their condition, men are avid for new sensations.

During the first period, Itard and Madame Guérin let the boy run through the full range of his moods and responses.

> One morning a heavy snowfall had begun before he had gotten out of bed. On waking, he uttered a shout of joy, jumped out of bed, ran to the window, then rushed back and forth between window and door. Barely dressed at all, he escaped to the garden. There, with great cries and bursts of laughter, he rolled in the snow and picked up handfuls of it. With incredible eagerness he wallowed in it and feasted on it.

But elation and excitement did not carry him away all the time. Often Itard observed a calm, almost meditative expression on his features and conjectured that the boy was having melancholy thoughts of loss and longing. This happened particularly when bad weather drove everyone else inside. The boy would go out into the garden, circle around the basin several times, and then sit down quietly on the edge. When moonlight entered his room at night, he often woke up, according to Madame Guérin, and stood for hours, watching the countryside "in a kind of ecstatic contemplation."

For several weeks Itard and Madame Guérin developed the boy's trust by letting him do exactly as he wanted all day long. It was a dream that could not last, of course, a special Garden of Eden prepared by his foster parents. Then the real work began. For if this animal was to become a human being, Itard and Madame Guérin would have to tease and nurse him and force him into retrieving his forgotten self from his earliest years.

> I had to gradually cut down his outings, reduce the size and number of his meals, make his nights shorter and his days both longer and more usefully employed in instructing him. In the long run I succeeded in doing so.

In the early stages of training Itard concentrated on two goals. He wanted to develop the boy's senses in order to make him more aware of his surroundings. And he wanted to interest him in simple games with people and things so as to sharpen his attention and his coordination.

Itard's account, echoing Bonnaterre's and Pinel's and Virey's, cannot be emphatic enough about how insensitive the boy appeared. In many situations he simply had no reactions. Cold weather and hot potatoes turn up again to prove that temperature barely affected him. Even filling his nostrils with tobacco didn't make him sneeze. During the worst mistreatment and misery in the early months at the institute, the boy had never been seen to cry. Except when they were directly connected with eating, he seemed not to hear sounds —at least to pay no attention to them. He moved, he was alive—yet he remained sealed off from almost everything. He responded with a fraction of his physical and mental faculties to the variety of the outer world. The rest of him, as far as Itard could tell, was extra baggage.

Itard began by having the boy take a hot bath every day for two to three hours, instead of letting him wander around the grounds. In his bath he behaved with the wonder and playfulness of a baby discovering water. He watched objects floating around him and laughed joyfully when water was poured over his head and coursed down his sides. "Before long," Itard wrote, "our young savage became sensitive to cold and used his hand to test the temperature of the water, refusing to get in his bath if it was not hot enough." This new aversion to cold had two effects: it made the boy stop wetting his bed, and it gave him a new interest in putting on clothes—for it was now midwinter in Paris. When left alone in his room with his clothes, he even began dressing himself. He also seemed to enjoy the massages Itard or Madame Guérin gave him after his bath. As they rubbed his small, scarred body, they were really reenacting the scene of Pygmalion trying to infuse human life into his statue. And we can imagine the Wild Boy beginning to become aware of his limbs, of someone else rubbing him and making soothing sounds, of himself responding to that person.

Among these new joys came outbreaks of irritation and anger. Itard noted them down carefully, for he felt that at those times the boy's intelligence took a step forward and found unexpected strength. He had reacted to something.

When Madame Guérin insisted on making him get into a bath he considered too cold, he first flew into a kind of tantrum and then, acting suddenly, took her hand and held it in the water to demonstrate his point. This was the same boy who had been unable to think of using a chair to reach an object too high for him. Itard takes special pleasure in telling one story. Itard had begun taking the boy to his own apartment in the institute for short periods. In his study he had a Leyden bottle, a primitive electric battery which could give mild shock. Having felt its effect, the boy was very wary of the device. One day, apparently to observe the boy's responses, Itard placed the Leyden bottle near him on the sofa and by pushing it nearer made him squeeze over into the corner till he could move no farther. He was also blocked by a table in front of him. Itard, seated on the other side of the bottle, reached out to take one of the boy's hands, which he had cautiously hidden inside his jacket. Caught in what looked like a trap, he moved very fast and took Itard totally by surprise. He pushed Itard's hand down on the bottle, and the doctor got the shock intended for the boy. Only quick, resourceful thinking could produce such a response.

The boy began to use a spoon to take potatoes out of boiling water. A hand mirror reflecting a ray of sunlight around a room would entertain him for a long time. He loved to run his hand over the corduroy material of Itard's clothing. Even his highly developed sense of smell seemed to improve, and Itard finally saw him sneeze. It was no small event.

> The fright he experienced when it occurred made me think it was the first time it had ever happened to him. Right afterwards, he threw himself down on his bed.

Is it possible that he had gone all those years without sneezing? Most remarkable of all, the boy developed both a marked fussiness about his food and a strong sense of cleanliness. All the earlier accounts describe how he had been content to live in filth and to eat filth. Now he began to refuse a whole plate of food if there was any strange substance in it. For Itard, the medical practitioner, the final proof of the boy's physical entry into the state of civilization was the fact that he caught a head cold and later two chest colds. (Bonnaterre had reacted the same way a year before.) As he tells it, Itard sounds proud, amused, and outraged that he had now undermined the boy's iron constitution.

All this took place, Itard states explicitly, in the space of three months. The boy was wakening to his surroundings. For the befouled animal to become finicky about dirt must have seemed a miracle. But certain other small details that Itard lingers over struck him as equally significant.

> If one got him to push or carry something, even something very light, he sometimes stopped suddenly and looked at the tips of his fingers. They could not possibly have been hurt or bruised, yet he would tuck them carefully inside his shirt.

The boy was discovering himself, becoming aware of his body, testing its parts and feeling twinges he had never felt before. We have all gone through the process, but so long ago as to have forgotten how much it means.

By putting all these little incidents together, we can begin to imagine what was happening inside the Wild Boy's mind. He was reaching a new awareness of something. In psychology there's a word for it; but the word will not create understanding, only hold it in place if we have already understood. Here's what the dictionary says:

cœnesthesia, n. The general sense of existence arising from the sum of bodily impressions.

The sensation of being alive as oneself. A million tiny events in our bodies and nerves and minds keep telling us that we are alive and how we are doing. We can be deaf to them, particularly if our survival depends on our not listening. That was the Wild Boy's initial condition, which continued for some time after he left the woods. He had existed without being alive—alive to the fact and the miracle of his own life. It was not so inappropriate after all that the boy had been sent to the Institute for Deaf-Mutes. For he had been deaf in the worst way of all. He couldn't hear himself; he couldn't hear himself living. And for three months Madame Guérin and Itard watched a thirteen-year-old boy come to life in front of their eyes, practically under their gently massaging hands.

Staying Home, Stepping Out

Itard worked wonders in developing the boy's senses of touch and taste. He tells us, however, that the boy's sight and hearing did not respond so readily. The boy probably gave that impression. He could see and hear well enough, but he simply didn't recognize most of the objects and situations around him in a building filled with people going about their business. And what he didn't recognize made no difference to him. In any case, the first two stages of Itard's program—to help the boy respond to other people and to train his senses—brought encouraging results.

Itard sets down the third stage of the boy's training as follows:

To broaden the sphere of his ideas, by giving him new needs and by multiplying his relations with the people around him.

Where Itard says "ideas," we would probably today say "perceptions." He wanted the boy to perceive not only more of his environment but also his relation to what was around him. As one reads this third section of the report and tries to picture the boy's behavior and state of mind at the time, one realizes that Itard's principal task was to stimulate or persuade the boy to *pay attention*—to find some kind of interest or participation in his own life. As Bonnaterre and Pinel had already reported, his most disturbing trait was his indifference to nine-tenths of what we consider the world, his environment.

Itard placed most of his hopes for catching the boy's interest and attention on games and toys. But in the first sentence he admits that he met discouraging obstacles right from the start. The boy simply wasn't interested in toys, even after Itard spent hours showing him how to play with them. He responded with impatience and hid or destroyed the toys if given the chance. Once, when alone in his room, he chucked a whole set of wooden ninepins into the fireplace and warmed himself before the flames. For a long time Itard could not change this pattern. Possibly the toys were too advanced for a child who still took pleasure in simple sensation like the feel of warm water or the grain of corduroy.

One activity did catch his fancy.

I set out in front of him several silver cups turned upside down. Under one of them I placed a chestnut. Sure of having caught his attention that way, I lifted them one by one except the cup with the chestnut under it.

Because he would never miss a chance to eat a chestnut, the boy became a sucker for the shell game. Itard made the game more complicated by using more cups and moving them around for a long time. The boy could almost always follow the moves and pick the right cup. Fearing that it was only greediness that motivated the boy to apply himself to the game, Itard substituted a pebble or an inedible object for the chestnut. The boy did just about as well and followed the game intently. Itard reflects sadly that, without the original chestnut, he might never have been able to draw the boy into the shell game. And he remarks on the enormous importance of children's games for the development of the intelligence. The way he speaks of his failure to interest the boy in other games makes clear that Itard had now met the first major setback in his program of instruction. And it came just when the boy's social and physical development looked promising.

Disappointed, but not discouraged, Itard tried other means of extending the boy's perception of what was going on around him. By February he was fairly well behaved. He would usually keep his clothes on, was trained to his chamber pot, could eat at a table, and didn't have to be kept on a leash. Therefore, the doctor could try taking the boy into the city for dinner at a friend's house. The first time, the boy appreciated the fine food so much that, before they left, he pilfered a plate of lentils from the kitchen and tried to take it back to the institute with him. Itard was delighted to see that these trips into Paris became very important for him—almost a need. Whenever Itard came into his room about four in the afternoon with hat and cane, carrying a clean shirt, the boy knew what was coming and got ready excitedly. Now it is true, as Itard states at this point, that a dog learns to recognize signs that he is going to be fed or taken out for a walk, and will jump around the way the boy did. But for the Wild Boy, who had been lower than a common dog to start with, the going-out-to-dinner game formed an important connection: good social behavior will be rewarded with excellent food. This practical training method led to some amusing scenes that Itard does not tell on himself.

One of the most beautiful, clever, and wealthy women of this period of French history was Madame Récamier. Almost all the prominent men of Paris—including the great romantic author Chateaubriand, and Napoleon himself—visited her château outside the city in Clïchy-la-Garenne. Still in her twenties, she received future kings, ministers of state, generals, philosophers, actors, astronomers, writers, foreign statesmen, and a few chosen women. In this brilliant salon, each guest was expected to give his best performance and then bask in the knowledge that he had reached the inner temple of celebrity and exclusiveness. Madame Récamier herself is usually shown in paintings reclining like a princess on her divan.

Anyone who became the talk of Paris was invited or taken to Madame Récamier's. That's the way the world goes. The rich get richer, and the famous meet the famous. Now, the Wild Boy of Aveyron was for a while the subject both of idle curiosity and of scientific interest. Both played a role in Madame Récamier's world. There is a wonderful (and not totally reliable) account, written by one of the ladies present, of the Wild Boy's visit to Clichy-la-Garenne, "accompanied by Monsieur Yzard [for Itard], who was his teacher, doctor, and benefactor combined." No question about which of the two was the celebrity. Having heard exaggerated stories about the Wild Boy, the elegant company was ready for anything, from the Noble Savage in person to a dangerous animal. Itard must have been nervous about the luncheon; this was not his usual company. But nothing flustered his pupil.

Madame Récamier seated the boy at her side, thinking perhaps that the same beauty that had captivated civilized men would receive similar homage from this child of nature. He appeared not yet fifteen. But the boy was not so gallant as the Huron Indian in Voltaire's novel [*L'Ingénu*] and too occupied with the copious things to eat, which he devoured as soon as his plate was filled. The young savage hardly heeded the beautiful eyes whose attention he had himself attracted. When dessert was served and he had adroitly filled his pockets with all the delicacies he could filch, he calmly left the table. No one noticed . . . Suddenly, a noise came from the garden, and Monsieur Yzard was led to suppose that his pupil was the cause. He got up to go verify his suspicions; our curiosity was aroused, and we all followed him in search of the fugitive, whom we soon glimpsed running across the lawn with the speed of a rabbit. To give himself more freedom of movement, he had stripped to his undershirt. Reaching the main avenue of the park, which was bordered by huge chestnut trees, he tore his last garment in two, as if it were simply made of gauze. Then, climbing the nearest tree with the ease of a squirrel, he perched in the branches.

The women, motivated as much by distaste as by a respect for decorum, kept to the rear, while the men set about recapturing the child of the woods. Monsieur Yzard employed all the means he knew to recall the boy, but without effect. The savage, insensitive to the entreaties of his teacher, or dreading the punishment that he thought his escapade deserved, leapt from branch to branch and from tree to tree, until there were neither trees nor branches in front of him and he had reached the end of the avenue. The gardener then had the idea of showing him a basket full of peaches, and nature yielding to this argument, the runaway came down from the tree and let himself be captured. He was covered up then as well as possible in a little dress belonging to the gardener's niece. In this outfit he was bundled into the carriage that had brought him and he drove off, leaving the guests at Clichy-la-Garenne to draw a sweeping and useful comparison between the perfection of civilized life and the distressing picture of nature untamed.

The Wild Boy was not invited back to Madame Récamier's. He was not yet ready for high society.

When master and pupil did go out, the boy traveled at such a fast trot that Itard found it easier to take him in a carriage than to keep up with him. That mode of travel produced even more thrills, and it revealed another marked change. On the trip from Rodez to Paris, the boy had barely reacted to coach travel; all he did was keep track of the food bag. Now he was delighted to take a carriage and he demonstrated his joy in every movement. One day when Itard took him out into real country to visit a friend in the lovely valley of Montmorency, the boy's pleasure seemed troubled by some new element.

> It was a very curious, and indeed a very touching sight, to observe the joy that showed in his eyes at the sight of woods and slopes in this attractive landscape. It almost seemed that his eyes could not take in enough of the scene through the carriage windows. He leaned out first on one side and then on the other, and became very uneasy when the horses slowed down or came to a halt.

During the two days they spent at this house in the country, all the boy's yearnings to return to the woods came flooding back, and special precautions had to be taken to prevent his escape. Itard speaks of him as "more impatient and savage than ever."

As a result, Itard did not take him to the country again. Instead, Madame Guérin took him almost every day for a walk or run in the garden of the Observatory, just next door. A family called Lemeri had a house there and the man or his wife often gave the boy a glass of milk during the afternoon. All in all, the Wild Boy began to become accustomed to his new life. "In the end," Itard writes, "he began to like it." He developed a genuine affection for Madame Guérin. Since Itard played the double role of taskmaster and protector, the boy's feelings toward him had many ups and downs. The account shows that within a few months the boy had accepted something approaching a family life. His devoted foster parents made demands on him and at the same time gave him security and an increasing amount of comfort. They even tried to interest him in sweet foods and wine. He learned to drink a little wine, but always preferred water. Unlike many domesticated animals, he would never touch sweets. The "state of nature" lingered on in unexpected ways.

A Name at Last

The last two sections of Itard's report are longer and more systematic than the first three. He did not begin this phase of the instruction until he had made several months' progress toward fitting the Wild Boy into the conventions of human society— at least into the way of life set up for him in the Institute for Deaf-Mutes. Looking carefully at what was demanded of the boy during these early stages—to take notice of his surroundings, to respond to people, to follow a schedule— one would have to conclude that the tasks he performed were not much more difficult than those required of a good sheep dog. He did wear clothes and could be persuaded to eat in company. But the major element was missing: communication in words. People talked and used sign language all around him. To talk *to* him was apparently a waste of time. For the boy did not hear (or see) words and paid no particular attention to voices except as noise or as tone of voice. He himself made no sound except for a few muffled cries and laughter.

Up to this point, Itard has described fairly steady and sometimes startling progress by the boy in spite of a few obstacles. He opens the fourth section with a sobering sentence which shifts the whole mood of his narrative.

> If I had wanted to set down here only my successes, I would have left this fourth stage of training completely out of my account.

Because he is a doctor, concerned with the outcome of this case and with the effectiveness of his training methods, Itard reflects at some length on why the boy did not master speech as rapidly as other skills. He first emphasizes that hearing the sound of the human voice is by no means the same thing as hearing the inflections of articulated speech and attaching meaning to them. He describes speech as "a kind of music to which certain ears, though otherwise normal, are insensitive." This selective deafness is found in "cretins," he states, meaning idiots. Does the Wild Boy suffer from such a defect?

I want to give Itard's full answer to this question and not quote just snippets. For this is the heart of the story. We have now come to a series of incidents that correspond to the moment in Helen Keller's life when, with her hand held under the running pump, she felt her teacher make one mark repeatedly in her palm. It is one of the most moving scenes in the history of education. At that moment something specifically human, something that links us all together, revealed itself more suddenly and dramatically than ever happens with a two-year-old infant. Helen grasped, simultaneously, the possibility of a code signifying our notions of things in the world and the meaning of the specific sign Anne was writing on her palm: water.

The Wild Boy's life traverses this same territory of meaning along a different path, and the comparison is worth keeping in mind. Unlike Helen Keller, he was neither blind nor deaf—not physically so, at least. In order to answer the question about a possible mental defect, Itard watched him very closely.

> This is what I noticed. In his first four or five months in Paris, the Savage of Aveyron reacted only to sounds connected with eating and escaping. By January he seemed to hear the human voice, and when two people began conversing in the hallway outside his room, he often went to the door to check that it was fully closed and then also closed the inside double door, checking the latch with his finger. A little later I noticed that he distinguished the voices of the deaf-mutes, or rather the guttural sounds they make while playing. He seemed to be able to tell where the sounds were coming from. For if he heard them when he was in the stairway, he never failed to run up if they came from below, or run down if they came from above in order to avoid them. By February I made a more interesting observation. One day when he was in the kitchen cooking potatoes, two people were arguing heatedly behind him without his seeming to pay the slightest attention. A third person came in who entered the discussion and began everything he said with the words: "Oh, that's different." I noticed that every time that person produced his favorite expression —"Oh!"—the Savage of Aveyron turned his head in that

direction. That night when he was going to bed, I experimented with various sounds and obtained approximately the same reactions. No other vowel sound seemed to have the least effect on him. This clear preference for the sound *o* led me to look for a name for him which ended with that vowel. I chose Victor.* The name stuck, and when someone uses it, he rarely fails to turn his head and to come running.

Possibly because it contains the same *o* sound, he soon came to understand the meaning of the word *no*. I often use it to correct the mistakes in his exercises.

Amid these slow but noticeable improvements in his hearing, he remained totally mute and refused to reproduce the articulated sounds which his ear appeared to discriminate. However, the external structure of his vocal organs showed no defect, and there was no evidence of internal damage. It is true that he carries a fairly long scar across the front of his neck, high up. It might raise questions about damage to the underlying organs were it not for the appearance of the scar. It looks like a wound from a sharp instrument, but being thin and straight the scar suggests a superficial incision that healed rapidly. It must have been the work of a frightened amateur, not of a hardened criminal. Left in the woods for dead, he probably recovered naturally from the wound, something that would have been far less likely to happen if the muscles and cartilage of the vocal organs had been severed. I conclude from these considerations that the boy's failure to repeat the speech sounds he was beginning to hear is explained not by some

* In French, the accent falls on the second syllable, and the *r* is barely audible. Therefore, the *o* sound is very pronounced. In choosing this name, Itard was also associating his young charge with the hero of one of the earliest and longest-running melodramas on the Paris stage, *Victor or the Forest's Child*, the work of the young dramatist Pixérécourt, adapted from a popular novel. Because of the success of those two works with the public, the name Victor was there waiting for the real Wild Boy.

organic lesion but by the unfavorable circumstances of his life. Total lack of use makes our organs incapable of performing their functions. If fully developed organs are so strongly affected by such disuse, what will happen to developing organs left completely untried? It takes at least eighteen months of careful education before an infant stammers out a few words. How could one expect that a rough creature of the woods, restored to society for only fourteen or fifteen months and five or six of those among deaf-mutes, could learn to speak? Impossible! In order to reach that important turning point in his education, he will require much more time and effort than it takes for even the slowest infant. An infant of eighteen months to two years may know nothing but he possesses to a high degree the capacity to learn everything: an innate tendency to imitate; great flexibility and sensitivity in all his organs; constant mobility of the tongue; and a larynx still of an almost gelatinous consistency. Everything contributes to his production of a constant burbling, an involuntary apprenticeship in voice formation supplemented by coughing, sneezing, and so on. Even crying helps. Crying demonstrates how sensitive the infant is to his own states. It also seems to spring from a strong steady drive in an infant to develop and coordinate breathing, vocal sounds, and speech precisely at the most opportune moments. Give me an infant to work with and I can guarantee the results. But Victor had none of an infant's advantages that I have just mentioned. He was already an adolescent. Still, one must also recognize Nature's resourcefulness in providing alternative means of education when accidental causes remove those she originally intended. Here, at least, are a few facts that justify this hope.

In the title of this fourth section I said I proposed to teach the boy to speak *by motivating him to imitate out of necessity*. I was convinced by the considerations out-

lined above, and by another circumstance that I shall describe in a moment, that I should expect very slow response from Victor's larynx. I would have to stimulate
it by using objects that answered his needs. I had grounds
for thinking that the vowel *o*, having been the first he
could hear, would be the first he would pronounce. It
was very favorable to my plan that this simple sound was
the sign of one of his commonest needs. [The word for
water in French is *eau*, pronounced as a clipped *o*.]
However, I was unable to obtain any results from this
lucky coincidence. Whenever he worked up a real thirst,
I held a pitcher of water in front of him and repeated
the sound *eau, eau*. While Victor watched, I gave the
pitcher to a person who pronounced the word, and asked
for it back in the same way. The poor boy writhed about
and waved his arms toward the pitcher in an almost convulsive manner. He kept making a kind of low whistling
noise but he formed no articulated sound. It would have
been inhuman to continue. I changed the subject, so to
speak, without changing my method. The next time I
tried the word *milk* [*lait* in French, pronounced approximately *leh*].

On the fourth day of this second attempt I succeeded
to my heart's content. I heard Victor pronounce, distinctly, though very crudely, the word *lait*, which he repeated immediately. It was the first time an articulated
sound came from his lips, and I found the greatest satisfaction in hearing it.

Later reflection, however, reduced the significance of
this initial success. It was only when, despairing of results, I had finally poured some milk into the glass
Victor held out that he had uttered the word *lait* with
great demonstrations of pleasure. And it was only when
I poured him another glass as a reward that he repeated
the sound. It is easy to see why this kind of result fell far
short of satisfying me. The word he pronounced, instead

of signifying a need or desire, was only a useless exclamation of joy associated with the moment at which he produced it. If Victor had said the word *before* he received what he wanted, my goal would have been accomplished. He would have grasped the true function of speech. A point of communication would have been established between him and me, and rapid progress would have followed. Instead, I had obtained only an expression of pleasure, without specific meaning for him and useless for me. At most, it was a generalized vocal sign of his possessing something. But, I repeat, it set up no relation between us, no communication. It would soon fall into disuse, since it did not serve his needs and depended on too many unlikely circumstances, like the brief feeling of pleasure with which he now associated it. The later results of this mistaken approach have borne out my fears.

In general, then, it was when he actually received some milk that he said the word *lait*. A few times he said it beforehand; and a few times afterwards, but always without any apparent purpose, without grasping its meaning. I attach little importance to the fact that he sometimes spontaneously repeated the word when he woke up during the night, and he may still do so. After these first results, I have completely given up the method I used to obtain them. While seeking a more effective method, I have abandoned his vocal development entirely to the influence of imitation, which is very weak in Victor, but not totally absent, to judge by few spontaneous advances he made soon after.

The word *lait* provided Victor with the basis of two other monosyllables, *la* and *li*. They had even less meaning for him. Only recently he has modified the second sound by adding a second *l* and pronouncing it as in the Italian *gli*, approximately *yee*. One often hears him repeating *lli, lli*, in a tone of voice not without sweetness.

It is astonishing that the liquid *l*, one of the hardest sounds for children to pronounce, should be one of the first sounds he produced. I am inclined to think that this difficult feat of articulation is Victor's way of reaching out toward the name *Julie*. Julie is Madame Guérin's twelve-year-old daughter, who spends all her Sundays with her mother. On that day one cannot help noticing that the exclamation *lli, lli* becomes more frequent. According to Madame Guérin's report, he even keeps making the sound at night when he appears to be sleeping deeply. It is very difficult to establish the cause and significance of this last development. To do it justice, we shall have to wait until his further growth into puberty furnishes more information. The latest accomplishment of his vocal organs has more meaning and is composed of two syllables—really three, the way he pronounces the second word.

It is the exclamation *Oh Dieu!* [Oh God!]. He has picked it up from Madame Guérin and frequently comes out with it when he feels happy. He pronounces it by eliminating the *u* in *Dieu* and doubling the *i*, so that one distinctly hears *Oh Diie! Oh Diie!* The *o* in this latest utterance is not new to him, for I had succeeded some time earlier in making him produce it.

This is where things stand in the attempt to train his voice. As you can see, all the vowels except *u* belong to his repertory of sounds, along with only three consonants: *l*, *d*, and liquid *l*. These are small accomplishments compared to what is required for the complete development of a human voice, but they strike me as sufficient to guarantee the possibility of that development. I have already explained why the process will necessarily be long and difficult.

There is one more contributing factor which I cannot leave out. Our young savage expresses his basic needs quite easily without words. Any wish on his part manifests itself in highly expressive behavior, in signs which have, as our words do, their relative values and their synonyms. When the time for his walk has come, he goes repeatedly to his window and to the door of his room. If he sees that his governess is not ready, he gets out everything she needs and in his impatience goes so far as to help her dress. After that he goes downstairs ahead of her and signals the attendant to open the gate. When he reaches the Observatory gardens, the first thing he does is to ask for milk [at the Lemeri house]. He does so by holding out his wooden bowl, which he always remembers to put in his pocket before leaving. The first time he did this was the day after he had broken a porcelain cup in which the Lemeris were giving him milk . . .

Was Victor acting like a mentally defective or retarded child? It does not seem so. Itard was being very demanding. He had every right to be pleased to get any articulate sound at all out of Victor's frozen vocal cords, and particularly by his spontaneous production and repetition of a few sounds. But Victor had no flash of understanding about meaning as Helen Keller did. Itard wanted the boy to *ask* for milk before receiving it; instead, Victor was apparently responding vocally to a generally pleasurable situation focused on milk. Itard's expectations were so high that he underestimated the boy's achievement. As a result, he failed to follow up Victor's first sounds and to encourage him to make more, as an enterprising parent would do with an infant. With time and experience, Victor might have refined the meaning of words and have moved from naming what was already there to requesting something in advance and evoking an absent object or idea.

Itard's last words in the section suggested that he understood the need for gradualness. For he compared Victor to "a child that begins by babbling the word *papa* with no clear idea of its meaning, saying it anywhere and any time, and later uses it for any man that comes in sight. Only after a series of deductions and abstractions does he begin to use the word correctly." But Itard did not apply the lesson that he states so concisely. For the time being, he gave up on teaching Victor to speak.

After the long passage on language quoted above, Itard goes on in the same calm style to describe a number of things Victor learned to do on his own. At their house in the Observatory gardens, the Lemeris used to entertain him by giving him a ride in a wheelbarrow. If everyone forgot about the game, Victor would go in the house, take someone by the arm, lead him out to the wheelbarrow, and get in. He usually got his ride. When he became hungry before dinner, he would set the table himself and get out the serving dishes. When he wanted to be served at table, he held out his plate, tapped on the serving dish with his fork, and, if ignored, would dump the whole dish into his plate. If visitors bored or annoyed him, he discovered that he could hasten their departure by presenting them with their hat and gloves and pushing them toward the door. Victor's pantomime was both expressive and entertaining. Itard insists that it did not correspond to mere animal behavior because Victor did not have to be taught the meanings of actions. Putting the boy to the test, Itard one day rumpled his own hair. With no further prompting, Victor went off to fetch a comb and gave it to his guardian. Estimating the importance of this "action language," Itard equates it with man's primitive form of communication before speech and the higher stages of culture. Victor's facility with action language probably slowed his acquisition of speech, for he could make his needs known with gestures. Itard and Madame Guérin also tended to use action language instead of talking to him constantly as one does to an infant just learning to talk.

Itard strikes a somewhat wistful note when he describes a child learning to say *papa*. He seems to be implying that before long Victor might learn that word and apply it to his young guardian. One of the first words Helen Keller learned was *Teacher*, a name more than it was a noun. Itard never mentions teaching a name for himself or Madame Guérin to Victor. However, the boy could hear some sounds, he had the pathetic beginnings of a voice, and he could express a wide range of emotions and desires through movement. In recognition of this nascent humanity, Itard gave him a name: Victor. But there was little of the conqueror about this boy. He had been better served by the humbler name Joseph when he was in Saint-Affrique.

Shock Treatment

The boy named Victor failed his speech course and disappointed his teacher. But Itard could not give up; he had taken full responsibility for the savage, and people were watching. Furthermore, there was one last step in Itard's training plan still to come: to develop and exercise the boy's mental processes. That meant working on his powers of attention and memory and judgment. Wasn't Itard wasting his time? At this point, it looks as if Itard's methodical habits of mind saved him from discouragement.

At the beginning of the fifth section, Itard states that, in respect to hearing, Victor was "little better than a deaf-mute." The institute where he lived housed about a hundred deaf-mutes, who spoke to each other all day long in animated sign language. They lived full lives, and often displayed intelligence, humor, and resourcefulness. Yet for some reason the doctor attached to the institute decided against teaching Victor to sign, or else the possibility did not occur to him. In any case, Itard does not mention it. Modern speech therapists and linguists tend to believe that Victor would have responded readily to a systematization of his action language into precise meaningful segments that he could share with others. What he could not hear in spoken language he would probably have seen in gestures. What he could not say with his paralyzed vocal apparatus he could probably have expressed with his hands and arms. But instead of choosing this path that seems obvious to us, Itard tried another.

Only a few months earlier Sicard, the institute's director, had published his book on how he trained the deaf-and-dumb Massieu to write understandable French in a year. Reading and writing seemed to be the explanation for Massieu's enormous success in making a life for himself outside the institute. After four or five months of trying his own schemes, Itard now decided to use the method of the distinguished man who had refused to educate the Wild Boy. If Itard saw the irony, he does not mention it.

In Sicard's training program, the student first learns to match a few simple drawings with the objects they represent: for example, a key, a hammer, a pair of scissors. A little later, when one drawing is pointed out, the student brings that object. Yes, a child can do it. But Victor was either too lazy, or too impatient, or too shrewd to play the game. When Itard pointed to one drawing, Victor did nothing, or sometimes he brought all three objects together.

Here was another dead end, it seemed. But Itard never ran out of ideas or hope. Making use of the remarkable fussiness Victor had developed about keeping things in their proper place, Itard changed tactics. In Victor's room he hung up a number of objects underneath simple line drawings representing them. When they had hung there long enough for Victor to associate drawing and object, Itard took the things down and gave them to Victor to put up again. This time he performed flawlessly, and repeated his feat several times—each object hung under its drawing. Then Itard saw what was happening. When he changed the arrangement of the drawings, it made no difference. Victor followed the original order and ignored the drawings. After that came several days of firm discipline by Itard and impatient wriggling from Victor. For the boy had to learn that it was not enough to memorize each set of positions (he could do that very quickly). He had to look carefully and match object and drawing. It is the first time Itard was able to provoke Victor into careful observation and comparison. He was almost thinking! Itard tells it all in a few lines which bury all the difficult human exchange that must have gone on in that small room between an uncooperative boy and a firm master. A ready imagination can turn these few lines into a whole scene.

His memory was doing all the work for him. I then concentrated on eliminating any possibility of his relying on memory. I succeeded in doing so by overburdening it with an increasing number of drawings and by frequently shifting the arrangements. After that his memory could not guide him in hanging up so many objects. What a difficult step I had just taken! I had no doubt of that when I saw our young Victor look carefully at each of his objects one after the other, pick out one, and then pick out the drawing that matched it. I soon verified the experiment by changing the order of the drawings. This time he hung up the objects in the new order.

The next step in Sicard's program was to place next to the drawing the word for that object. Here again, Itard passes over what must have been weeks of exasperating work, all in vain. Victor saw no connection between the unfamiliar shapes of letters and either the objects or the drawings. Itard finally realized that he was asking for too much too soon. Deaf-mutes could make the leap because "of all children they are the most attentive and observant." Not so Victor. It must have been a blow. Victor couldn't learn to talk. He couldn't equal the performance of the deaf-mutes in learning to read simple words. Was Victor deficient, after all? At this point, Itard does not even raise the possibility. But he must have had terrible doubts about ever leading the boy any closer to communication and intelligence. Whatever his thoughts were, Itard gave up the Sicard method and developed "my new plan." The methods and devices Itard invented at this point to train Victor's "still sluggish faculties" are probably the best demonstration of his imaginativeness as a teacher and of his willingness to return to fundamentals. He realized that Victor did not distinguish simple shapes and colors. How, then, could he "see" words or even letters? Itard started his pupil on a set of exercises so effective that they are used today in kindergartens all over the world.

On a piece of paper two feet square Itard glued a red circle, a blue triangle, and a black square. A cardboard cut-out of exactly the same colored figure was hung above each of the three. After a few days Itard took the cutouts down and Victor hung them back up in the right places with no trouble. Changing the arrangement of the figures did not throw him off. A few days later he could match the three shapes all of the same color, and three different colors of the same shape. Now Itard began adding more colors and shapes: for example, an intermediate shade of blue and a parallelogram.

Victor made only a few mistakes and seemed able to learn new items within a few days. Clearly, Itard was excited.

These results emboldened me to make further changes, each one more difficult. Every day I added new elements and took some out. I shifted them around and kept insisting on new comparisons, new judgments. In the end these exercises became so numerous and complicated that they fatigued his attention and his cooperativeness. At this point Victor began to display the reactions of impatience and anger that had come out violently when he first arrived in Paris, especially when shut up in his room. Nevertheless, it seemed to me that the time had come not to calm these outbreaks by giving in to him but to overcome them by resolute action. I decided to insist that he do what I wanted.

And so things reached the point where, disgusted with a task whose purpose was beyond his grasp and which quite evidently fatigued him, he would spitefully throw the pieces of cardboard on the floor and retreat to his bed in a fury. After a minute or two I would begin again as calmly as possible. I made him pick up all the cardboard pieces scattered around the room and would not let up until he had correctly placed every one of them.

My insistence worked only for a few days, and in the end his independence of character won out. His outbreaks of anger became more frequent and more violent and resembled the fits of rage I have already referred to. But they were directed less against people than against things. In this destructive state he rebelled by chewing his sheets and blankets, biting the mantelpiece, throwing andirons, ashes, and burning coals around his room. He would then fall into convulsions. As in an epileptic fit, he would end up by losing consciousness. When matters reached this frightening stage I was forced to give up. Yet my yielding only made matters worse. The attacks came more often, and could break out at the slightest frustration, sometimes for no apparent cause.

I was extremely upset. I kept imagining that all my training would only transform the boy into a pitiful epileptic. A few more attacks like that and the sheer force of habit would set the pattern of one of the most dreadful of incurable diseases. I had to find a remedy without delay—not some medicine of doubtful value, not gentleness, which had already proved ineffective, but some form of shock treatment, like the one Boerhaave used in the Haarlem hospital in Holland. And I was convinced that if my first attempt failed, his illness would only get worse and any similar treatment would become useless. Therefore, I chose the method which I believed would be the most frightening for a being who, in his new existence, had experienced no form of danger.

Some time before, Madame Guérin had taken Victor up to the roof of the Observatory. It is very high. When he was still some distance from the parapet, he took fright and began to tremble all over. He ran back to his governess, his face covered with sweat, and dragged her by the arm toward the stairs. He did not calm down until he had reached the bottom. What had caused such fright? I never tried to find out. All I needed to know for my purposes was his reaction. The right moment soon came when, by starting the exercises with the cardboard cutouts again, I provoked one of his most violent fits. Acting swiftly before he lost consciousness, I threw open the window, which was on the fifth floor, with a stone pavement down below. Looking as furious as I could, I seized him forcibly by the hips and held him half out the window with his head directly over the drop. When I brought him in a few seconds later, he was pale, covered with cold sweat, tearful, and trembling a little from what I thought must be fear. I led him back to the work table. I made him pick up all the cutouts and match them properly. He went through it all, slowly, it's true, and not too well, but without impatience. Then he threw himself on his bed and wept.

This was the first time, at least to my knowledge, that Victor had ever cried . . .

This curious treatment succeeded—not completely, but well enough. His resistance to the work did not disappear entirely, but at least it lessened and never again led to the kind of reaction I have just described.

If he became tired or if he had to work at times usually set aside for his walks or meals, he went no further than to show his uneasiness and impatience and to make a kind of plaintive muttering that usually ended in tears.

This change for the better allowed us to pick up the exercises where we had left off. I modified them again in order to reinforce his powers of judgment. For the cutouts of geometrical figures I substituted line drawings of the same figures. To ask him for colors I used irregularly shaped samples with no resemblance to the colored cardboard pieces. The boy had no trouble with these new difficulties. I had now accomplished what I wanted in adopting the method of direct comparison. The time had come to replace it with a more instructive approach, which would have been totally impossible for him if I had not prepared him for it with the exercises he had just performed successfully.

It must have taken courage as well as imagination to scare the wits out of the boy in order to cure his tantrums. That day Itard could have lost his wager, after only a few months. But the shock treatment worked, at least after a fashion. The game was still on, with higher stakes than ever. We can only guess what psychic changes may have taken place within the boy as a consequence of this shock. He had been subdued.

Had Itard also broken his spirit in some way? Even the later events of the story do not give a clear answer to that question. The scene reveals the deep tensions that had grown up between pupil and teacher. "I was extremely upset." That is the strongest language Itard ever uses to describe his feelings. It sounds as if the two of them never missed a day's work.

Itard now set out to teach the chastened Victor the letters of the alphabet. They used a board divided into twenty-four compartments. The twenty-four large letters of a specially printed alphabet could be distributed among the compartments. There were also twenty-four metal cutouts of the letters for Victor to place in the right compartments. Itard was much impressed by the fact that right away Victor learned a trick for doing the exercise without learning the letters. When the boy took the metal letters out of the spaces, he went in order across the rows and stacked them carefully in his hand. To put them back, he simply reversed the order. If he didn't drop the letters, he could do the whole board this way. Itard states that this "routine" may have displayed as much inventiveness on Victor's part as learning to recognize the individual letters. Afterwards, he did learn the letters and could match them faultlessly. Itard made sure to shift the order around so that Victor was not just memorizing positions.

At this point, more out of curiosity than in expectation of any result, Itard laid out the letters LAIT on the table. Madame Guérin, after looking at them, gave him a glass of milk. Then Itard gave the four letters in random order to Victor and held up a glass of milk. The boy proceeded to make the word, but in reverse order: TIAL. He had seen it upside down. Itard corrected the word and gave him the milk. Hard as it is to believe, Itard writes, Victor learned to spell out the word LAIT in five or six tries and also seemed to understand "the relation between word and thing."

Itard thought he had good evidence for making that claim. A week later, before leaving for the Observatory gardens, Victor picked out those four letters of his own accord and took them with him. When he reached the Lemeris' house, he produced the letters and spelled his word on the table. Itard tells it very softly, with no fanfares. But that day Victor must have received some warm hugs and encouragement.

After nearly nine months he had used his first word—not just an exclamation of pleasure but a rudimentary means of saying something to someone else in conventional signs having no resemblance to the object designated. It looked as if he had finally surpassed action language.

The First Report

Though it had happened some time earlier, Itard holds this story about forming the word *milk* until close to the end of his first report. Other things had developed more recently, such as Victor's halting attempts at speech with the sounds *gli* and *Oh Dieu!* But for Itard, looking at Victor's whole course of development after months of training, nothing could match the accomplishment of putting down four letters to spell LAIT. He valued this "last result" so highly that he decided to let it stand in place of a summary at the end of his report.

First of all, Victor had learned directly from his training to recognize shapes and letters and then to grasp that one set of letters could mean or name a specific thing. The second consideration is even more important. Outside the routine of his training exercises, impelled by an association of ideas and possibilities that no one had suggested to him, Victor had spontaneously picked out four letters and carried them into a completely new setting in order to compose the word for milk. For the first time, it appeared that Victor had run ahead of his teacher. He had seen for himself what could be done with the materials around him, as if he had had the idea of using a chair in order to reach something too high for him. Itard had obviously been holding himself back in the earlier parts of his report. This spontaneous behavior by Victor convinced him that his diagnosis had been borne out and that the boy's condition was by no means incurable.

I calculate that it was in June or July that Victor used the metal letters to spell out LAIT. At least it was in June, seven months after Pinel's diagnosis of idiocy, that Itard attended a meeting of the Society of the Observers of Man with Sicard and was eagerly questioned about his work with the Savage of Aveyron. Avoiding the questions, he agreed instead to write a report for the Society. Until then he had made no public statement of his disagreement with Sicard and Pinel about the boy's condition. In his careful handwriting he finished the seventy-page report in two months and read it to a meeting of the Society on August 26, 1801. By October, it had been printed and officially presented to the Society.

Though the last three pages do not summarize the stages of Victor's progress, Itard comes to the following conclusions about his condition:

> The boy known as the Savage of Aveyron is endowed with the full use of all his senses; he gives constant proof of attention and memory; he can compare, discern, and judge, and can apply all his faculties of understanding to the objects employed in his training.

What had struck everyone at the beginning, and Pinel above all, was the boy's failure to take an interest in anything except food. Itard insists many times on Victor's newly acquired ability to pay attention, on his alertness. The ironic result of this change, of course, was to remove the very characteristics that made the boy exotic and "wild" at first. In a long footnote on the next-to-last page, Itard points out that anyone who had not observed Victor when he first arrived in Paris would be unimpressed with him now and see "only an almost ordinary child, who doesn't talk." Itard means that Victor now dresses, walks, looks around him, responds, and generally behaves himself in no way like a "savage." Whatever ordinariness Victor had attained served to demonstrate the "truly immense distance" he had traversed in nine months. Itard invites any "enlightened observer" to come and see for himself.

It seems odd, here at the end of his first report, that Itard tucks those important claims about his success with Victor into a footnote. But the sentence that opens the next paragraph takes a great leap forward and reveals what is really driving Itard. "Think of the significant conclusions about the philosophical and natural history of man that result from this first series of observations!" Notice the exclamation point; Itard was not in the habit of getting excited. Claiming that he has produced "material proof" of the ideas of Locke and Condillac, Itard now lists five "important truths" which he feels have been demonstrated by Victor's development. I give them in modern terms:

1. In the state of nature—that is, running wild as this boy did, without social organization as we know it—man is inferior to many animals.

2. Man's superiority comes out only in the state of civilization, which raises him by appealing to his powerful sensibility. That sensibility shows itself principally in two drives: the desire to *imitate* and the desire to *innovate* or invent.

3. The imitative faculty, an essential factor in speech learning, loses its strength at an early age, particularly under isolated conditions.
4. The innovative faculty develops in direct relation to the number of needs an individual feels. Thus, increasing our needs multiplies our ideas and contributes to the development of a higher state of knowledge and civilization.
5. Medicine and the natural sciences must encourage the education of these faculties in order to improve the human species.

Itard produced these ringing claims about the nature of man and his basic faculties soon after the close of a century that believed in progress and, in fact, almost believed it invented progress. He was concerned not only with training Victor but also with what that training demonstrated about the "perfectibility" of the human species. The Wild Boy of Aveyron had only two basic needs: food and sleep. Itard decided that the creature could be humanized if he developed other needs—the need for warmth and comfort, the need for human company and exchange, the need for play and distraction, and more. In other words, Itard set out systematically to corrupt everything "natural" about the boy's initial way of life. He succeeded. Victor was someone else, a person wearing clothes, alert to his surroundings, orderly in his habits. After this nine-month crash course in civilized behavior, Victor had developed a limited yet recognizable sensibility. The observations Itard goes on to make about imitation and innovation dig very deep. First of all, his statement that the ability to imitate (and through it the ability to learn to speak) will wither away if it is not exercised and reinforced anticipates present-day theories about a "critical period" or age before which certain mental faculties must be developed. There may be a double bottom of meaning in the old proverb, "You can't teach an old dog new tricks." Furthermore, I find in Itard's use of the term *sensibility*, calling it a "powerful motive force" in human beings, an attempt to define the instinct for self-preservation in us as a constant exchange between imitation and innovation, between conformity and liberation. Human life requires both in a dialectic of opposites. Itard's thinking here virtually implies that the exclusive pursuit of either term—conformity leading to paralysis and boredom, or liberation leading to rootlessness and excess—represents a form of destructiveness, of what Freud called the death wish. Thinking about human nature in Victor leads Itard into deep water, and draws us after him.

Today Itard's fourth point about increasing our needs seems wrongheaded if carried too far. When everyone in a developed society "needs" an automobile and a television set, we have advanced an immeasurable distance beyond Victor's condition. We see the population running over and natural resources running out, and we conclude that we must *reduce* our needs. But these recent consequences of progress after a century and a half of technology should not blind us to the soundness of what Itard wrote about the lessons of the Wild Boy of Aveyron. The reduction of our needs to zero produces a form of death; the multiplication of our needs within certain social and personal constraints seems to favor both culture and self-fulfillment. The fine adjustment of our needs and desires to the world around us runs like a refrain through the writings of Montaigne and Rousseau, Goethe and Freud.

In 1800, most men still tended to believe that the basic elements of a person's life are fixed at birth, that heredity decides our temperament, intelligence, moral fiber, and talents, and probably our social and economic status as well. For a century, however, many philosophers had prepared the ground for a new position based on the *tabula rasa* and emphasizing environment and education over heredity. Preaching liberty, equality, and fraternity, the champions of the French Revolution set out to change the rigidity of status that seemed to hang over every human life. We are still deeply engaged in that struggle. Itard showed not the slightest interest in political or revolutionary ideals. He had simply read his Condillac about how sensations gradually fuse into useful knowledge; he pursued his medical training conscientiously; and he worked with a savage boy whose lot in life seemed the lowest and most desperate imaginable.

What was Victor's heredity? No one knew, nor have we ever found out. Itard answered the question by assuming that the Wild Boy of Aveyron was a test case of heredity, the lowest common denominator, a being approaching human putty because he had never been stimulated to develop needs and desires. Modern biology tells us that the genetic code written into every cell is more complex and powerful than anything Itard grasped. However, he had some justification for thinking that Victor represented heredity bared to the bone, stripped of the cultural layers that overgrow it in almost all human beings. He believed he had found the dog beneath the skin.

From all these ideas and from Victor's development under training, Itard drew a revolutionary conclusion for his day: *education is all.* An individual human being has greater potential than we usually acknowledge. Carefully planned, steadily applied training using a mixture of reward and command can achieve remarkable results from unpromising material. By applying this method with love and understanding, Itard transformed a savage humanoid animal into a tractable and likable boy, still without speech. The young doctor implied in his first report that the human species is almost infinitely perfectible, or at least infinitely malleable. Today a group of vocal and influential psychologists declare very much the same thing. They speak of "operant conditioning" or "behavior modification," an almost mechanical system of training that can be applied to any individual to change his ways and, above all, to problem children and some mental cases. Itard has been seen as one of the pioneers of behavior modification, of both its theory and its techniques. But, unlike the modern fanatics, he never lost touch with the individual human beings under his care. The difference is crucial and probative. Behavior modification, based on conditioned reflexes and related to brainwashing, sets out to manipulate individual deviations in favor of a selected norm, usually social. Itard did not aim at any such flattening out of behavior through conditioning reflexes. He addressed himself to the whole individual. In the fifth conclusion at the end of the first report, he speaks with conviction of how education and modern medicine can cooperate effectively in perfecting the human species "by appraising and appreciating the organic and intellectual anomalies *in each individual* and by determining what education should do for him and what society can expect of him" (italics added). The training Itard developed for a particular deprived individual, the Wild Boy of Aveyron, is only distantly related to behavior modification as a method. On the other hand, Itard's work stands as a major precedent for the broad area of activity known today as "special education."

Itard states his position about education and "socialization" not only at the end but also in the foreword to his first report. The opening paragraph with its clear echoes of Rousseau on the state of nature may sound a little flowery to us, but he is laying his cards right on the table.

> Cast into the world without physical strength and without innate ideas, unable by himself to obey the laws of organized behavior that set him above all other creatures, man achieves the high place marked out for him in nature only within a social setting. Without civilized society, he would be one of the weakest and least intelligent of animals. Though often affirmed, this truth has not yet been rigorously demonstrated.

What we call "savage" peoples, Itard goes on, have already been raised and trained within a certain cultural pattern. They tell us nothing about the totally uncivilized state of man. The so-called wild or wolf children found in the woods in the seventeenth century tell us little more, for most of the accounts are unreliable and unscientific. But now that modern medicine and modern philosophy have developed sound methods of observation and training, we should be able to reeducate such a savage child if found, or at least to measure the "till now unreckoned sum of knowledge and ideas attributable to a man's education."

Those, Itard states in his foreword, are precisely his goals in undertaking to train the Wild Boy of Aveyron. It is still too soon, he says, to produce final results demonstrating his claims about education and society. But after nine months he feels he has "proved" this much:

> The boy from whom I have obtained these first successful results is by no means, as is generally believed, an incurable imbecile, but on the contrary an interesting being who deserves careful observation and special care from an enlightened and philosophical government.

This is Itard's reply to Pinel's and Sicard's original diagnosis. The facts as he gives them in the following pages seem to support him.

In the last two paragraphs of his report, Itard mentions a matter he has not discussed earlier. According to everyone's estimates, Victor was thirteen or fourteen at this point. In 1800 there was little talk about adolescence and none about "teenagers." The word commonly used for this stage of growth was *puberty*. It did not designate a long period of waiting and semi-dependence while going to school and training for work and a full place in society. It referred to a clear line between childhood and maturity, marked unmistakably by the appearance of the secondary sex characteristics in both boys and girls. Even clothes do not hide that change; they often emphasize it. It does not happen overnight, yet it does not take the six or seven years fenced off by our teenage-adolescent category. Puberty usually means a year or two.

All known societies have ways of directing the physical and mental energies released by puberty toward approved forms of work, play, and social conduct. Without those constraints, the young would fly off in all directions, and the community would suffer. Sometimes, after puberty, the young enjoy a period of initiation, permissiveness, or privilege—"rites of passage" or "sowing one's wild oats." Western societies then focus all drives—economic, emotional, sexual, reproductive, social—on one unit: the family. No other institution, except perhaps an extended series of schools attended, competes with the family as an organizing principle for human energies.

The Wild Boy of Aveyron was captured at the onset of puberty. He was undergoing certain physical changes and disturbances just when Itard set about to train him and to redirect his energies. By bringing in Madame Guérin, Itard placed Victor in a semi-family situation. That arrangement appears to have led to genuine human attachments and to have stabilized Victor's behavior somewhat. Unfortunately, Itard doesn't deal specifically with the effects of puberty until the very end of his report; one can only glimpse between the lines the restlessness and exasperation it caused. It must also have been nearly impossible to distinguish puberty from mere animality in the boy; everyone continued to call him the "Savage" in French. In any case, Victor's puberty, coming on top of the original trauma of abandonment and his isolation over a long period, added another complicating factor to make his training difficult.

Other sources supply a little more information. In the fall Victor seems to have become attached to a young girl whom he met in the Observatory gardens. One weekly newspaper following his case described Victor's behavior toward her as a mixture of devotion, fear, and obedience interrupted by constant distractions. Very little had occurred in his life to direct his lusts or his longings toward "the other sex." In fact, all accounts imply that he had little opportunity or encouragement to form an idea of another sex, or to see himself as male. Romantic love with its ideal of intense emotion concentrated on one person was surely beyond his ken. With a few inevitable exceptions, Victor did not know either the "facts of life" or the social forms through which we approach them. After nine months in civilization he still apparently had no sense of shame or modesty about any bodily functions or activities.

It is in this light that we should read Itard's last paragraph. He felt that Victor's behavior as a still unsocialized creature threw into doubt some of our most sacred beliefs about love and sex.

Dr. Itard, benefactor of the Institute for Deaf-Mutes. The lithograph shows Itard approaching forty, several years after he discontinued his training program with the Wild Boy. (Photo Bibliothèque Nationale)

The Wild Boy of Aveyron, age twelve or thirteen. The only authentic portrait that has survived, used by Itard as frontispiece for his first report in 1801. The original caption: "Showing on the front of his neck a transversal scar due to a criminal attempt on the boy's life." (Photo Bibliothèque Nationale)

The Wild Boy of Averyon: contemporary engraving. The mythology surrounding the boy's capture inspired imaginary portraits like this, showing him in the wilderness with long, claw-like nails, but neither hairy nor naked. (Musée Fenaille, Rodez; photo Balsan)

The Institute for Deaf-Mutes, Paris (ca. 1846). (Photo Bibliothèque Nationale)

– l'ensemble de mon travail. une occasion extraordi-
– naire se présenta de l'employer à des études
accessoires, et d'un intérêt tout nouveau. il –
s'agissait d'observer sur un enfant muet, non sourd,
élevé loin de toute société humaine le développement
tardif de l'instinct de l'imitation, l'influence
de l'imitation sur le développement de la
parole, et de la parole sur la formation et
l'association des idées.

Une grande partie de mes journées fut
pendant six ans sacrifiée à cette minutieuse
expérience. Cet enfant qu'on appelait le
Sauvage de l'Aveyron ne recueillit pas de
mes soins assidus tous les avantages, que j'en
avais espérés. mais les observations nombreuses qui
s'offrirent à moi, les procédés d'instruction
que me suggéra l'inflexibilité de ses organes

ne furent pas entièrement perdus, et j'en fis plus tard
une application plus heureuse chez quelques uns de nos
enfants dont le mutisme tenait à des obstacles
moins insurmontables.

The extraordinary opportunity
presented itself to devote my time to related research
with a whole new range of interest. It
was a question of observing in a mute boy, not deaf,
raised far from all human society, the delayed development
of the instinct of imitation, the influence
of imitation on the development of
speech, and of speech on the formation and
association of ideas.

A large portion of my days
for six years was sacrificed to this demanding
experiment. The boy, who was called the
Savage of Aveyron, did not gain from
my attentions all the advantages I had
hoped. But the numerous observations
I was able to make, the instructional procedures
suggested to me by the intractability of his organs,
were not entirely lost, and later I put them
to more successful use in dealing with
children whose muteness arose from
less insurmountable causes . . .

Autograph manuscript by Itard on the Wild Boy. In 1825 Itard wrote a report to his superiors at the Institute, inserting a succinct passage on the Wild Boy—the only text on the subject that survives in his own handwriting. Twenty years after the events, it gives Itard's measured opinion of the case and of his contribution to science and education. (Institut National de Jeunes Sourds, courtesy of L. Dessaint, Headmaster)

*Sicard among his students. This painting by Langlois (1808) shows
Sicard instructing a pupil, not to speak in sign language, but to produce
speech sounds by responding to the sense of touch. (Institut National de
Jeunes Sourds, courtesy of L. Dessaint, Headmaster)*

[A lack of sufficient facts] has prevented me, in this discussion of young Victor, from emphasizing the onset of puberty. Within the past several weeks it has displayed itself in an almost explosive fashion, and its first manifestations throw much doubt on the origins of certain affections of the heart which we regard as very *natural*. I have had to refrain from coming to hasty conclusions. And I remain convinced that only time and further observations can confirm all the considerations that tend to destroy certain prejudices or opinions, many of them respectable, and that are among the most attractive and consoling illusions of our social life.

Precisely what was Itard referring to in those closing words of his report? He never explained himself, not even to the Society of Observers of Man, which asked him for clarification. Victor's actions seem to have convinced Itard that much of what we think of as instinctive in sexual behavior and love has to be learned by human beings. "Boy meets girl" may not come naturally; even here, education is all.

Those enigmatic sentences at the close of Itard's report sound a somewhat ominous note. He was a little worried about his charge and shows it. However, there are other passages that appear earlier in the text but belong to the last few weeks of this stage of Victor's training. They sound more hopeful about his emotional responses. Generally Itard spends little time describing his own relation to the boy and the attachment that grew up between Victor and Madame Guérin. At the end of the third section, however, after recounting how difficult it was to persuade Victor to play games and engage in activities that might develop his intelligence, Itard speaks about the walks Madame Guérin took with the boy to the Observatory gardens. The events reported here are recent. Those exchanges and rituals must have sustained Victor as a developing human being. He did have feelings toward the two persons who took care of him and who were bringing him back to his own estate as a man. The following passage reveals more than any other the warmth that had grown up in that family of three: Itard, Madame Guérin, and Victor. It is the only time Itard shifts this way into the present tense. Here is both the heart and the unacknowledged conclusion of his first report.

One time, when he escaped from Madame Guérin in the streets, he shed a great quantity of tears on seeing her again. Several hours later, he was still sobbing and had a very high pulse rate. Madame Guérin then said some reproachful things to him. He understood her tone of voice so well that he broke out crying again. The feeling of friendship he has for me is far weaker, and that is as it should be. All the things Madame Guérin does for him he can appreciate right away; he cannot see the usefulness of the things I am doing for him . . . Yet at times I too am welcome. They are the times I have never used for any kind of instruction. If, for example, I go to his room at nightfall when he has just gone to bed, his first movement is to sit up so that I can hug him, and then to draw me to him by taking my arms and making me sit on the bed. Then he usually takes my hand, places it over his eyes, on his forehead, on the back of his head, and holds it with his own in these places a long while. Other times he gets up with bursts of laughter and places himself opposite me where he can caress my knees in his special way. He squeezes them and rubs them hard for several minutes in all directions, and sometimes touches them with his lips two or three times. People can say what they want, but I admit that I go along with all this childishness and don't interfere.

Perhaps I shall be understood if people remember the major influence on a child of those endless cooings and caresses, those kindly nothings which come naturally from a mother's heart and which bring forth the first smiles and joys in a human life.

CHRONOLOGY 1800–1806

The Wild Boy

1800:   Jan 9: captured in Saint-Sernin (Aveyron)

        Jan. 10–Feb. 4: held in Saint-Affrique orphanage

        Jan. 25: letter about boy in Paris *Journal des débats*

        Feb. 4–July 20: kept by Bonnaterre in Rodez Central School

        August 6: arrives in Paris, Institute for Deaf-Mutes

        August–Nov.: publicity, neglect, uncertainty

        Nov. or Dec.: Itard begins training sessions with boy

        Dec. 31: Itard appointed resident medical officer at Institute for Deaf-Mutes

---

1801:   Jan.–Feb.?: Itard names the boy Victor

        June: convulsions and "shock treatment"

        July: Victor forms the word LAIT (milk)

Dec. 1799:   Society of Observers of Man founded

March: opening in Paris of *The Savage of Aveyron or Don't Swear by Anything,* vaudeville show

August: Bonnaterre publishes *Historical Account of the Savage of Aveyron*

Fall: Sicard's *Course of Instruction for a Deaf-Mute*

Oct.:   Pinel's *Treatise on Insanity*

Nov. 29:   Pinel's committee report to Society of Observers of Man: boy described/as an idiot

---

May: Pinel reads conclusion of his report to Society of Observers of Man. Boy diagnosed as imbecile

August: Itard reads his first report on Wild Boy to Society of Observers of Man and sends copy to Minister of Interior. State funding renewed

1802: ear training; Victor discriminates sounds, including human voice
special exercises in visual perception and motor imitation; Victor
learns to draw shapes and letters
training of touch; Victor learns to concentrate and to relate touch
to sight
eye training; Victor learns to recognize and reproduce a few
words formed of metal letters, and learns their meaning

1803: Victor uses written words "spontaneously"; Victor "invents" a
chalk holder; adjustments in Victor's grasp of words

1804: Itard tests Victor's "sense of justice"; training in oral articulation
and production of speech sounds through imitation is a failure

1805: Victor's puberty "crises" disrupts work and discipline; end of
regular training

1806: May: Madame Guérin's appointment and salary renewed by
Minister of the Interior

May 3: Sicard reports to skeptical Minister of the Interior (Chaptal) on the boy's progress: state support continued

---

Itard completes his medical study with a thesis on pneumothorax

---

June 13: sympathetic Minister of the Interior (Champagny) asks Itard for a detailed report

Sept. 15: Itard delivers his second report

Nov.: Itard's work is commended and the report ordered published at government expense

4

Man-Plant or Moral Man?

Back to Basics

Itard was not a man to stand back. A fledgling doctor aged twenty-five, he set out to do what the experts said could not be done. In nine months he tamed and trained the boy they called a hopeless idiot. In his report, however, Itard did not crow too loudly about his accomplishments. He just glowed, and described Victor's training with no embellishments and full acknowledgment of failure in some domains. The report in the summer of 1801 proved his point about the Wild Boy of Aveyron as fully as was necessary to defend his reputation. After that, he could easily have claimed that his work was done and turned Victor over to someone else, or to Madame Guérin alone. But the passage I have just quoted reveals the depth of his feelings for this boy, who was almost more his creation than a true son of his could have been. This bachelor had an offspring.

And now Itard faced the question of how to go on. It is worth recalling the Wild Boy's story as Itard had formed it in his mind. The boy grew to about the age of six in unknown conditions. He was probably normal, though he may have been severely deprived or disturbed. When abandoned, he became completely wild and survived alone for five or six years in the forests around Lacaune and Roquecézière. After capture, he spent five months under the care of Bonnaterre and Clair in Rodez. Then, following the initial interest in his case when he arrived in Paris, came three months of neglect in the Institute for Deaf-Mutes. Itard took over at that point and worked with him for nine months, leading up to the first report.

The next stage encompasses five years. During most of that period Itard does not appear to have slackened his efforts to train the boy or to have modified his basic faith. He continued as resident physician at the institute. The government paid for Victor's board and lodging and for Madame Guérin's services and a small, five-hundred-franc, annual stipend to Itard. One member of Pinel's committee, Degérando, wrote a favorable review of Itard's report when it was published in the fall of 1801. Degérando expressed considerable doubt about Pinel's diagnosis of idiocy and stated that the progress Itard had made with the boy reinforced those doubts. He also brought out that Itard "has developed a completely new kind of education" in order to achieve his success. This was only one small voice, however. The Wild Boy of Aveyron had disappeared from the news and gossip of Paris. Itard worked on virtually alone—but not quite.

In May 1802, fearing that the Minister of the Interior would cut off state support for Victor, Sicard wrote a letter describing the boy's training under Itard and predicting further progress. The letter represents a surprising change in Sicard's position: the director of the Institute for Deaf-Mutes now appears to support Itard and oppose Pinel's original view that the boy was an ineducable idiot. Even Pinel shifted his ground somewhat. This support must have encouraged Itard. The information contained in this letter combined with Itard's final report of 1806 yields a fairly clear version of the events in Victor's life between 1801 and 1806. Itard's euphoria expressed in the 1801 report did not last long.

He decided to develop several of Victor's senses at the same time, particularly hearing as "the sense that contributes most directly to the development of our intellectual faculties." He meant thinking and talking. He also realized that in order to remove Victor from constant distraction, he would have to isolate this one sense and concentrate on it.

Sometime in the latter part of 1801, Itard blindfolded Victor and gave him a bell and a drum. When Itard banged the drum or rang the bell, Victor was to do the same. The boy distinguished the sounds with little difficulty. These serious play sessions must have made an odd sight. Later, by holding out the proper finger, Victor showed that he could also recognize the sounds of various wind instruments and finally the full range of intonations of Itard's voice. There seemed to be nothing faulty about this boy's hearing. On the contrary, he began to love these sessions. He had found his sport.

Yes, either because he really enjoyed hearing the sound of the human voice, or because he liked being blindfolded for hours on end, several times during our breaks he came up to me with his blindfold in his hand, held it around his eyes, and began to jump for joy when he felt me tying it behind his head.

Itard encouraged what he thought were favorable signs, and went on to work on the five basic vowel sounds in French. Victor was supposed to hold out a different finger for each vowel. This process should have required a far greater degree of concentration and discrimination than anything so far. Instead, Victor kept bursting out in "attacks" of joy and laughter. It was just a game to him. He got nowhere with the vowels, and finally in despair Itard removed the blindfold to calm him down. Immediately everything in the room, especially any movement, distracted the boy and interrupted the exercise. The blindfold had to go back on. Itard became very severe and rapped Victor's knuckles with a drumstick to stop his foolish laughter and correct his constant errors. The effect was greater than Itard had expected—and so was his own reaction.

Tears trickled down from under the blindfold, and I hastened to take it off. But, out of embarrassment or fear or absorption in his own feelings, he kept his eyes closed even though the blindfold was off. I cannot describe the pained expression on his face with his eyes closed and every so often a tear coming out between the lids. Oh! at that moment as at many others when I was ready to give up the task I had imposed on myself and when I looked on all my time as wasted, how deeply I regretted ever having known this child, and how I condemned the barren and inhuman curiosity of those men who first uprooted him from an innocent and happy life!

This scene put an end to my pupil's noisy gaiety. But I had no reason to be glad of the result, for I avoided that obstacle only by running into another. Fear took the place of gaiety, and our exercises fared even worse. When I pronounced a letter, I had to wait more than a quarter of an hour for his response. Even when he gave the right answer, he did it so slowly and uncertainly that the slightest movement or noise on my part made him pull back his finger. Afraid of making a mistake, he tried another finger with the same slow apprehension.

After these long sessions, attempted from time to time in later months with no greater success, Victor learned to recognize only a few monosyllables expressing anger or sadness or friendship. Victor just was not ready, or able, to hear language as spoken to him, and fear of punishment probably stifled his participation.

This failure placed Itard in a quandary. How could Victor ever talk if he couldn't hear the sounds normal children seem to learn effortlessly? For Itard, vocal speech was the principal test of the whole rehabilitation experiment. The boy wasn't deaf; why should he remain mute? It was through working with Victor that Itard learned about the varying degrees of hearing impairment, knowledge he later applied to help deaf-mutes.

During this time Itard had continued Victor's visual training with metal letters. "After several months of work my pupil knew how to read and write passably a series of words some of which differed very little from one another." "Read and write" claims too much. Victor was assembling metal letters into the groups we call words, or recognizing them on a blackboard. *But they had no meaning for him; he could not even pronounce them.* "Reading" was still a long way off.

And there was another factor, something that seemed to

deflate what Itard had held up in his first report as Victor's greatest accomplishment. Five or six correct uses of the letters LAIT had been enough, he thought, "to give Victor an idea of the relation between word and thing" (see page 106). In the conclusion of the report he cited this step as a "guarantee" of the boy's future progress. Sometime later, Itard noticed several disturbing things that obliged him to think again. How does language mean something to us? He refused to deceive himself about what his pupil was really accomplishing, and these pages of his later report provide a lucid statement of elementary linguistic principles.

> No matter how much Victor wanted some milk, it was only at the moment when he was accustomed to receive a glass, just when it was being given to him, that he said the word, or rather formed it out of the metal letters.

Victor would not produce the word in order to obtain milk at other times. He spelled out LAIT only when he was sure of being able to obtain it. Exactly the same thing had happened in his attempts to articulate the sound *lait* (see page 94).

Itard perceived two serious flaws in the way Victor used his first word. First, Victor could not detach the word from the presence of what it meant—from its "referent." There is no true language without that separation. Second, what *lait* referred to for Victor was extremely imprecise. Clearly it did not mean "white liquid produced by a female mammal, anywhere, any time." His behavior suggested something closer to: "my pleasure in drinking this white water, right here, right now." Itard watched his triumph turn to ashes.

> I concluded that his use of the word, instead of being an expression of his needs, was merely a sort of preliminary exercise which he went through mechanically before sat-

isfying his appetite. We would have to retrace our steps, therefore, and take a different path. I resigned myself with the best courage I had, convinced that the fault was mine and not my pupil's.

Thinking about the causes for his defective use of written signs, I had to acknowledge that my first exercises with words and ideas did not have the extreme simplicity that had led to the success of my other teaching procedures. It meant that even though for the rest of us *lait* is a very simple sign, for Victor it might be either a confused expression of this nourishing liquid or of the receptacle it came in or of his desire to drink it.

It is hard to tell when Itard had these doubts about what he had considered Victor's greatest triumph. Probably it happened in early 1802, at about the period when Itard decided that the time had come to teach Victor how to draw the letters and write the words he could now recognize and form out of metal cutouts. The decision led to a revealing incident. Itard set Victor up beside him at a blackboard with a piece of chalk to follow his teacher's movements. But it didn't work, and Itard says he expected as much. *Victor didn't know how to imitate.* He seemed to lack the elementary faculty that becomes very powerful in young children, the double process of seeing an action and doing likewise. Of course, Victor had great difficulty seeing what we see. Yet many animals imitate; all languages have verbs like *ape* and *parrot.* If Victor had had the ability and the desire to imitate people around him, he would probably have educated himself much earlier. In his first report Itard had stated that Victor's capacity to imitate was "weak but not extinguished." Now he discovered just how weak it was.

Once again Itard set out to reawaken responses that had

gone to sleep years before in the boy. "I had to retrace my steps and lift his imitative faculties out of their inertia by gradual training. I started on a program of obvious movements for him to reproduce, like raising the arms, advancing one foot, sitting down, standing up, opening and closing the hand, and a series of simple finger movements that could then be combined." Later, watching his tutor, Victor grasped a stick in his hand and wielded it like a big pencil, thus strengthening his muscles. It sounds infantile and it was, infantile and essential. Itard does not say how long the exercises lasted—several months, I estimate.

Finally the two of them could stand again side by side at the blackboard. This time, Itard reports, "The result of our performance was two parallel lines." Sicard's letter of May 1802 opens with a description of Victor reproducing both large figures and small letters. He had learned a new skill.

Itard also worked on Victor's sense of touch. At the start Victor couldn't tell a chestnut from an acorn when he had to choose one or the other from the bottom of a bag or jug. Months of carefully graded exercises trained his fingers to distinguish not only objects and shapes, temperatures and weights, but even the metal letters. In this area he was a willing and rapid student.

Itard decided to leave the boy's sense of smell alone as already sensitive enough. But taste was another matter. In 1800 a cultivated Frenchman believed that to discriminate and enjoy good food constituted a vital part of "civilization." Would the Wild Boy come to this? Itard must have appreciated the irony of what he was attempting, for he wrote that he set out "to develop, or to pervert" Victor's organ of taste. This time Itard does not describe the training methods he devised but comments at some length on the results. The two passages make a nearly perfect pair.

In getting used to new tastes and dishes, Victor remained indifferent to strong drink. This indifference changed into real aversion as the result of a mistake he made that is probably worth describing. Victor dined with me in town one night. At the end of the meal he picked up of his own accord a carafe of a strong liqueur that was clear and colorless. Having poured himself a glass of what he took for water, he thirstily drank off half of it before the burning sensation in his stomach told him what he had done. Throwing down both glass and carafe, he went out the door in one leap and began to run howling up and down the halls and stairs of the building, coming back in and starting out again on the same course, like a wounded animal . . .

Itard finds special significance in Victor's preference for water.

Almost always when he has finished dinner, and even when he feels no great thirst, Victor will fill his glass with pure water, assuming the air of a gourmet getting ready to taste an exquisite liqueur. He sips it slowly and swallows it drop by drop. But what adds even more interest to this scene is the place where it happens. Our refined drinker goes to the window and stands with his eyes turned toward the open country. It is as if at such a moment of enjoyment this child of nature wanted to reunite the only two possessions that have survived his loss of liberty—a drink of clear water and the sight of sun and countryside.

The passage edges toward poetry—one sensitive temperament observing another with deep empathy. Only a few pages earlier Itard was cursing this boy for his failure to learn vowels.

One of the by-products of this extended period of sensitivity training turns out to have been very important. After the

fiasco of ear training, Victor's capacity for paying attention
and his alertness developed beyond the level Itard had described in his first report. He began to fix his eyes on what he
was doing. It made all the difference. Remembering that the
boy's inability to focus on anything "led to the original suspi-
cion of idiocy," Itard carefully describes Victor in the process
of learning to concentrate. Some of these exercises in perception absorbed him completely and caused a "serious, calm,
meditative expression to spread over all his features." Itard
almost paints the "Savage" as a budding philosopher.

Reading and Writing

Itard now believed that Victor was ready for the next stage
of training. If the theories of Locke and Condillac were correct, the boy had formed two series of notions in his mind as
the result of the exercise and development of his senses. He
had a "crowd of new ideas" about the world and himself; and
he had a set of potential "signs," particularly words made out
of letters, to represent those ideas. The *tabula rasa* had received these marks, but without as yet any systematic association between the two series. *Lait* was an exception, almost a
fluke. The value or meaning of the signs belonged not to the
senses but to a higher level of mental activity. That was the
next step in Itard's program.

We would not describe things this way today. As we see it,
Victor's mind, not just his senses, had been at work in some
non-linguistic fashion even before he was captured. Sensations and impressions do not organize themselves spontaneously; some potential for making sense of things, for arrang-
ing impressions into categories of space, time, and cause-effect
seems to belong to the earliest stages of human life. The Wild

Boy had coped well enough to survive without help in a harsh environment. His mind had not been totally inactive. By the time he was captured in Saint-Sernin, he had evolved a rudimentary action language, expressing his basic needs by pointing and acting them out. But Itard was by no means wrong in breaking down the training process into stages to make sure that all fundamentals had been properly learned. Victor probably was beginning to have ideas distinct from his needs. (That, of course, is the hardest thing to know.) But he could not convey those ideas in any adequate way. Consequently, he may have felt more alone than ever. Drinking water by the window could have expressed this loneliness. Months before, Itard had sensed this heightened isolation in Victor. When the boy first produced a semblance of the sound *lait*, Itard realized that it was more a blurred "exclamation of joy" than a word. "It established no relation, no communication between us." But now, after months of work on perception and discrimination, Victor looked ready for a new attempt by Itard to establish just that communication.

If Itard's judgment was right, the next step should be simple. "It was necessary . . . to establish between each object and its sign a direct connection and a kind of identity that would fix them in his mind." Sicard's method for deaf-mutes had already produced partial results (see pages 100–3) and could now be used again. Itard laid out in a set of bookshelves various objects each placed on a card carrying its name. Victor had already learned in earlier exercises to distinguish all these words by sight; he did not yet know their meanings. Two years before, when Victor had been expected to match object and word, the results were nil. This time he caught on so fast that Itard barely describes how it happened. "This setup was quickly grasped. I had proof of it when, after changing the order of the cards, I watched my pupil place each object on the right word." This time he could *see* the words and link them to things.

A few hitches developed. Itard began sending Victor out of the room to fetch an object whose name he pointed to. At first Victor had to keep the written name in sight to get the right item. Without that reminder, he forgot the word very quickly and would come back to check. But after a time he became quite proficient. He could go upstairs to get four different things at once, remembering them accurately and even dawdling along the way to look out the window. And finally something entirely different happened. "I saw Victor, both in our exercises and spontaneously, making use of the words I had taught him, asking us for things, fetching them or pointing them out when he was shown the word, or pointing at the right word when given the thing." *Spontaneously*: it looks like the key word in the sentence. Victor was almost working on his own. Itard felt that he had "finally arrived at the point for which he had retraced his steps and made so long a detour." It was the breakthrough. It had taken two years.

As Itard tells it, never an up without a down. One day when he was working with Victor in his study he decided to lock the door so that Victor could not go to his own room, where all the objects had been put that he was usually sent to fetch. Instead, he could find the same items (book, key, knife) in Itard's study. But though there were scores of books staring him in the face, he would not settle for any of them. He wanted to get the usual one locked in his room. Itard could not persuade him to link the words on the cards with any of the objects there in the room. Itard describes himself as losing all patience.

"Unhappy boy," I burst out as if he could understand me, "since all this work has been in vain, go back to your woods. Or since you're now a ward of society, face up to your own uselessness and go live out your time in Bicêtre in misery and boredom!" If I hadn't known the limits of my pupil's intelligence, I might have believed that he understood every word I uttered. For I had barely finished when I saw, as happens in such moments of sorrow, his chest begin to heave with sobs, his eyes close, and tears stream out of his lids.

In response to this behavior, Itard did something that seems both very natural and very calculated, as if he could be a loving father and a detached clinician at the same time. From past experience, he believed that these emotional crises were "salutary" for Victor. The shock that cured his tantrums the first spring seemed to improve his learning performance. Itard now went over to hug the boy and comfort him with words. At that, Victor let all his feelings go. "I carried his emotion to the fullest limit and, so to speak, tried to touch the innermost fiber of his moral being." After a while, they began to work again, and things went better.

A new series of exercises taught Victor to associate classes of objects according to their properties and uses, instead of always differentiating between individual things. Victor learned quickly that BOOK meant not just the one particular book they had been using but all sheets of printed paper bound in a cover. Then he went through a state of overcorrecting and generalizing too much. He confused BRUSH and BROOM, KNIFE and RAZOR. To demonstrate the latter distinction, Itard shaved himself while Victor watched. Once pointed in the right direction, Victor was able to associate objects by similarities and to make distinctions, and then to use words as a means for remembering these categories of things.

At this point Victor was outdoing himself. Itard shows his

excitement in the next section by stepping out of the narrative for once and addressing himself directly and by title to "Your Excellency," the Minister of the Interior, for whom he was writing the second report. Itard insists that Victor now discovered the faculty of imagination.

> I have no hesitation about giving that name to the way he made himself a chalk-holder. One day in my apartment he had used such a device for holding stub ends of chalk. A few days later the same situation arose when he was in his own room with no holder to use. I put it to the most inventive of men to guess what he did then—or to do as much themselves. Victor picked up a little kitchen implement that didn't belong in his room and had therefore been tossed to the back of his closet. It was a *lardoire*, used to insert fat into a roast. It could do the job he wanted, and in a second burst of creative imagination he turned it into an effective chalk-holder by replacing the slide with a few turns of string. Please try to understand, Your Excellency, why I attach so much importance to this deed. One would have to go through this whole painful course of instruction, follow and guide this man-plant in his laborious growth, from his earliest moments of attention to this first flash of imagination, to form an idea of the joy it afforded me. Pardon me for making so much of so simple and ordinary a discovery.

Victor began to use his wits for all kinds of little discoveries like this, as if the basic process of learning to use words accurately had liberated his whole mind to deal with the world around him.

> From that moment on, he dropped spontaneously a whole set of routines and habits he had picked up in

performing his assigned tasks. Without drawing unwarranted conclusions, I think that one could say that this new way of looking at things, and its new applications, forced my pupil to break out of the circle of automatic or mechanical behavior.

Things moved very fast for a while. Victor learned words for entities fairly difficult to conceive, like *room* or *person*. And he had no difficulty understanding that the parts of a thing could have names distinct from the name of the whole. Then came adjectives like *big* and *little, soft* and *hard, hot* and *cold, light* and *heavy,* and many more qualities and colors. Finally, verbs: *touch, throw, pick up, drop, drink, eat,* and so on. Itard combined them with the nouns, and Victor had a whole series of acts to perform. The master had his pupil scurrying around the upper floors of the institute like a demon. When the random lists of words produced odd combinations like "tear stone" or "eat broom," Victor wasn't thrown off by the absurdity; he made some sensible substitution. All this went like a house afire. Victor could still not talk or understand oral speech. But language now vibrated in all his actions. And Itard had kept after his writing.

I shall report only that, after several months, Victor knew how to copy the words whose meaning he already knew. Soon after, he learned to reproduce them from memory and finally to use his writing, crude as it was and still is, to express his needs, to ask for what he wants. By the same means he can grasp the needs and wishes of others.

Itard uses no exclamation points, no italics here as he did at the close of his first report. But the tone is optimistic. Unfortunately, none of Victor's written texts have survived.

Early in 1803, as I interpret the chronology, Victor learned the basics of reading and writing. He could communicate spontaneously in a crude fashion. Along the way, he had almost stumbled into two major accomplishments. The part of his intelligence we could call imagination or invention had begun to operate in this new setting. And he had learned or relearned the faculty of imitation. For Itard there was only one path to take now: vocal speech.

If Only He Could Speak!

Itard wrote his reports with great thoroughness, but there are some important details he omitted. Victor did not distinguish spoken words, but he did understand tones of voice. Did Itard and Madame Guérin continue to talk to him as we talk to an infant even though it does not understand the words? Or did they allow vocal speech to lapse except for expressive fragments like *no, good, come here, again, faster,* and so on? To what extent did they develop a basic language of gestures? Itard never writes of trying to teach Victor to sign the way deaf children did who lived all around them. A sentence in Sicard's 1803 letter informs us that sign language was occasionally used on Victor, but never systematically. In my imagination I see Madame Guérin talking to Victor constantly as to a child, and Itard working with him in relative silence. But there is no clear evidence to support this picture. In any case, Itard had not given up on speech; he had been biding his time.

Having worked for months with Victor on distinguishing vowel sounds and all in vain, Itard knew that the boy could neither hear speech sounds adequately nor reproduce them. He stated that Victor was the mental and psychological equivalent of a born deaf-mute. There would be little point in trying to teach him to speak by the normal means of repeating sounds if he didn't really hear them. But Victor had acquired two new abilities since his training started: he was observant and he could imitate what he saw. Itard realized that there was another method to teach him to speak: not through hearing, but through sight.

> This last effort meant training Victor to see and to understand the mechanism by which we make articulate sounds, and then training his vocal cords to reproduce them . . . For more than a year all my work and all our exercises were aimed at this goal. In order to arrange the process in carefully graded steps, I had him first imitate the most obvious and pronounced movements of the face muscles. And there we sat, student and teacher facing one another, grimacing away at each other, making the most outlandish movements with our eyes, mouths, foreheads, jaws, and all our other face muscles. Gradually we concentrated on lip movements, and then on the tongue. All this went on for a long time, through all imaginable variations.
>
> Prepared in this systematic fashion, Victor's speech organs seemed to me ready, beyond a doubt, to imitate articulated sounds. My hopes were totally disappointed. All I could obtain from this lengthy training was a few blurred monosyllables, some shrill, some deep, and much less clear than the ones I had elicited in my earlier attempts. All the same, I kept on for a long time, in spite of Victor's response. Finally, seeing that my efforts were leading nowhere, I gave up my attempt to teach Victor to speak, and I abandoned him to a state of incurable muteness.

Thus, in one page, Itard describes the longest and most sustained single sequence of training—well over a year, and probably running into 1805. Some of the scenes of the two making faces at each other may have been amusing at first, but such games pall before long. Somehow they kept at it, yet it all led to Itard's most discouraging defeat. He had tried carefully to follow methods and principles that he had applied with great success to other aspects of Victor's education. Victor's period of greatest response and progress, when he learned to read and write, immediately preceded his most unexpected failure. What happened? The two paragraphs quoted above suggest to me that Itard was still expecting Victor to hear sounds that his ear could not discriminate.

In any case, for the first time an impasse had been reached. Before this point, it had always appeared to Itard that a carefully designed program of training, a willingness to return to basics, plus superhuman patience and resourcefulness, would finally overcome all obstacles and restore Victor's lost capacities. For Itard finally to accept the fact that he could not teach the boy to speak marked a change in the entire relationship. Ironically, we know that at this period Itard had begun successfully training some partially deaf children at the institute to speak by these very methods. Victor seemed deafer and muter than before.

Growing Up Half Tame; a Theory of Justice

Itard's faith in Victor's humanity was immense, sturdy enough to sustain five years of demanding work. In order to reach the boy's mind and release its presumed powers of thought and imagination, the doctor had concentrated— properly, I would say—on language. We have seen the results: no speech, not even in the conventional signs of deaf-mutes; only a rudimentary understanding and use of written words.

Like a glass which is both half full and half empty, Victor's verbal training had ended in success or failure according to one's point of view. But beyond any evaluation of the results lies the deeper, darker question: Who was Victor now that he had been partially awakened from the sleep of isolation? Had the wild creature incapable of attention or reflection developed into a person with feelings and character? All those tears of Victor's, and Itard's occasional outpourings of joy or despair, imply a genuine relation between two people deeply attached to one another. Itard organized his second report to reply to precisely such questions. The title of the third section uses a term still current in psychology to refer to the emotions: "The Development of the Affective Faculties."

In certain ways Victor had not thrown off the call of the wild.

> It's always the same passion for the country, the same rapt ecstasy at the sight of a beautiful full moon, or a snow-covered field, and the same transports when a windstorm comes up. His passion to roam freely in the fields has been tempered by his new social attachments, and partly satisfied by his walks. But the passion has not been extinguished. It takes only a beautiful summer evening to revive it, or the sight of a shady woods, or any interruption in his daily walks.

We would do well to reflect on such a passage and set it beside the earlier description (page 132) that associates landscape and drinking water. Does this behavior signify a lingering wildness or savagery in Victor? Or does this deep-seated appreciation of landscape at specific moments display a rudimentary form of aesthetic sensibility he had developed by himself before capture? The two impulses may have been linked. Victor's association of beholding beauty in the landscape with savoring pure water verges on a mythological combination of themes of purity.

When Bonnaterre and Clair had brought the boy to Paris five years earlier, he clearly recognized his two keepers and behaved docilely with them as the people who supplied his basic need for food. But did he return Clair's affection? Itard states that when Clair left there was no observable response on the boy's part. However, as time went on, he became increasingly eager to perform well for Madame Guérin and Itard and even to be of service. He responded to encouragement and did some useful work. One of the tasks he liked most was sawing wood.

> You can watch him redouble his efforts as the saw cuts deeper. When he actually saws through, he acts out an extraordinary demonstration of joy. One would almost be tempted to compare it to insane delirium. Yet his behavior can be explained by a need of movement in this active being, and by the nature of the activity, which, in addition to being a healthy and stimulating exercise, offers him the opportunity of making himself useful by doing something that pleases him.

Though he may hold it in check, an ordinary fifteen-year-old boy will not be unfamiliar with such a wild response to physical exertion.

The reverse side of exuberance is depression. Victor experienced it increasingly. After long and concentrated effort, especially in learning words, he was sometimes unable to surmount a difficulty. "I have seen his tears begin to fall on those incomprehensible letters, provoked by no word of reproach from me, by no threat of punishment." The tantrums of the first year had been left far behind. Itard's careful training methods were designed to avoid unnecessary mental frustrations. In any case, the boy seems to have understood much of what was going on around him and what was expected of him. One of his daily chores was to set the table for Monsieur and Madame Guérin and himself. In 1804 or 1805, Monsieur Guérin fell seriously ill and was cared for elsewhere. Victor kept on setting his place, and each time Madame Guérin had him remove it. Monsieur Guérin did not recover. The day of his death, Victor set his place as usual.

> One can imagine the effect this had on Madame Guérin. After witnessing her outpouring of grief, Victor understood that he had somehow brought it on. Either because he thought he had done something wrong, or because he grasped the real reason for her grief, Victor saw that his action was out of place. Of his own accord he removed the place setting, put everything back in the cupboard, and never set it again.

Itard relies principally on two incidents to portray Victor's emotional development. About the time of her husband's death, Madame Guérin went to bed for two weeks with bad rheumatism and could not take Victor out for his walks. He was overjoyed when she recovered and could barely wait for their trip to the Observatory gardens. But the first day Madame Guérin left the institute she could not take Victor with her. That evening at dinner when he was sent to the kitchen to get a dish of food, he went out into the courtyard, slipped through the big gates of the institute while a carriage was coming through, and escaped to the fields. The police in a village some distance away captured him and held him for two weeks before he could be identified and returned to Paris to be claimed by Madame Guérin. Apparently, several people witnessed the event.

As soon as Victor saw his governess he became pale and lost consciousness for a moment. When he felt Madame Guérin kissing and caressing him, he revived quickly and expressed his joy in shrill cries, convulsive movements of his hands, and a radiant expression on his face. To the onlookers he looked less like a fugitive brought back by force to captivity than like an affectionate son who of his own accord throws himself into his mother's arms.

He showed no less feeling in his first meeting with me the next morning. Victor was still in bed, and he sat up as soon as he saw me and held out his arms. But when he saw that instead of going up to him I remained standing in front of him, with a cold bearing and an unhappy expression, he plunged back under the covers and began to cry. My strong reproaches made his sobs redouble. When I had stimulated his feelings to their limit, I went to sit down on his bed. That was always the sign of forgiveness. He understood, made the first advances of reconciliation, and all was forgotten.

For a scientific case history, this book describes a lot of weeping. Itard makes it clear that Victor's strong emotions do not spring just from having missed his usual comforts for a few days. We also find confirmation that Itard talked to Victor, but that the boy understood only his tone of voice and his actions.

The second incident probes deeper into Victor's training and Itard's methods because it raises the question of what ideas of right and wrong were forming in the boy's mind. The tacit understandings we live by are at stake here, the cement that holds a society together. Itard begins his account in his usual quiet tone. Gradually he works up to a warm celebration of the potential nobility of man. No matter how one interprets these incidents, I find no reason to ridicule either Itard's or Victor's responses.

When Itard first took charge of the Wild Boy, the boy had no sense of property. He openly picked up anything he could lay hands on—principally, things to eat. Punishment taught him only to hide his acts—that is, to steal; he filched food constantly from the kitchen. Then Itard was obliged to confront him with the beginnings of moral conduct in the form of the golden rule reversed. If Victor stole something, Itard took something from him, if possible an item he particularly coveted, like bread given him as a reward for good work. These "reprisals" taught the boy that if he was going to steal from others, others could steal from him. His thievery finally stopped.

But Itard was not satisfied. He could not determine whether Victor had mended his ways out of mere fear of reprisal or out of an "inner sentiment of justice . . . a disinterested sense of the moral order." It is hard to tell how seriously Itard expected to find those elevated and subtle sentiments after two or three years of training. How many ordinary citizens, at fifteen or any other age, have developed a genuine sense of justice and act by ethical principles rather than because of fear of the law? Novels and newspapers are full of cases of people being put to the test. Itard's account verges on the melodramatic.

In order to find out what was really going on in my pupil's mind, I decided to test him with a form of unjust punishment. Since it would not be provoked by his actions, it would appear totally undeserved, an odious and revolting act. For this truly painful experiment, I chose a day when I had kept Victor steadily at work for over two hours. Satisfied with both his cooperativeness and his intelligence, I owed him nothing but praise and rewards. And he expected as much, to judge by the happy look on his face and the whole posture of his body. You can imagine his astonishment when, instead of receiving the customary rewards that he had every right to expect from me, he saw the severe and threatening look on my face. I violently rubbed out the writing I had just praised and threw his cards and notebooks all over the room. Then I took him by the arm over to the closet in which I had locked him up a few times as a punishment soon after he arrived in Paris. He let himself be led to the closet door. Then, suddenly throwing off his usual docility and bracing his hands and feet against the door-frame, he struggled against me vigorously in a way that gratified me because it was so unlike him. Never, when he deserved such a punishment, had he resisted. I persevered now, in spite of everything, in order to see how far he would carry his resistance. Mustering all my strength, I got ready to lift him bodily into the closet. This maneuver roused all his anger. Red and outraged, he fought so violently in my arms that for a few minutes I couldn't do anything. Then, feeling himself about to give way to my greater strength, he called on the last resource of the weak. He bit into my hand hard enough to leave deep tooth marks in it. How wonderful it would have been at that moment to be able to make myself understood to my pupil, to tell him how that pain filled my soul with satisfaction and repaid me for all my trials! Do I have a right to be pleased with what happened? His was an act of legitimate retaliation. It gave incontestable proof that the sense of justice and injustice, the eternal basis of the social order, was not foreign to his heart. In giving him this sense, or rather in encouraging its development, I had raised a savage to the full stature of moral man.

It is worth thinking awhile about this scene. Itard sees it as Victor's rite of passage to the estate of man. The boy had learned the difference between right and wrong and now he had had the courage to protest against the wrong even in the face of his tutor's deeply established authority. Most of us would want to be more guarded in our language than Itard, but how would we phrase it? I would go this far. Victor had not become so browbeaten and dependent that he could not react strongly when his expectations, or his "principles," were violated. Perhaps he was merely expressing confusion over a sudden return to a form of punishment long abandoned. Still, Itard's self-congratulation appears to be based on an accurate observation that the boy perceived "something wrong" in the punishment and was impelled to react vigorously. Could a person go through years of training without learning to distinguish deserved reward or punishment from arbitrary and undeserved treatment? I doubt it, not if the tutor were as fair-minded as Itard. An animal trainer has to follow a consistent, not a whimsical program. An extended set of successful social transactions, as between Victor, Itard, and Madame Guérin, has to be founded on some predictable pattern of behavior and response. To call that pattern "justice" implies the need for consistent predictable actions.

Itard tested Victor that day and found the pattern alive and strong in him. It was a verification of past progress, not a sudden giant step forward. Victor cannot have had in mind any clear concept of justice in the abstract, or any word with which to express it. He could not have generalized the basis of his reaction in this "experiment" to different situations that touched him less directly. In an important sense, therefore, Victor had not attained the "full stature of moral man." Nevertheless, Itard had good reason for celebration. Victor had caught on to the unspoken rules of human exchange and had not lost his independence of spirit. Though "odious," the scene demonstrates the strength of their relationship, and it apparently did not interrupt or complicate the training program.

We have now seen Victor at his peak. Though mute, he had learned to "read" and to convey simple ideas by writing. He felt genuine affection for his foster parents, Itard and Madame Guérin. He had enough imagination to invent small recombinations of parts of his environment. Finally, he seemed to have a rudimentary notion of justice based on right conduct. Why wouldn't this responsive creature, who had been a mere animal a few years earlier, go on to become the noblest of men? After his long isolation, would he produce some privileged wisdom about the development of human consciousness, like the man born blind who recovers his sight? Some such notion seems to have sustained Itard.

Yet at a point toward the end of the second long stint of training, probably in 1804, Itard must have realized that Victor's progress was not picking up but slowing down. The first nine months in 1801 had produced a near-miracle. Then for a long period Itard's perseverance and resourcefulness had found a way around every obstacle except Victor's incapacity to hear and to produce articulated sounds. Finally, at a stage that cannot be pinpointed accurately, Victor's restless behavior forced Itard to evaluate the boy's situation all over again. And now he found two apparently insuperable obstacles. One was the absence of an essential element or trait that had never developed; the other was the presence of a natural force that could not be channeled or put to good use. These factors bring the experiment to a close by revealing Victor's limits and by reviving the specter of bestiality and savagery. Itard was stumped, and he says so, reluctantly but frankly. The following passage comes only a few lines after the scene about justice.

Victor has remained essentially egotistical. Full of eager-
ness and friendliness when the duties one assigns to him
are in line with his own needs, he remains a stranger to
that willingness that gives no thought to hardship and
sacrifice. He does not yet know the sentiment of pity.

Victor an egotist? Doesn't this contradict the whole significance of that scene in which he opens up his heart after running away? No, because he obviously identified Madame
Guérin and Itard with the satisfaction of his needs and desires. Itard mentions *pity* here. Rousseau believed that pity
was the one spontaneous emotion a primitive man would feel
in the state of nature. Itard was probably familiar with Rousseau's thought. But he refers to pity basically because it sur-
passes egotism. Pity is a kind of spontaneous justice. It
depends on one's being able to imagine another person's suf-
ferings and to be affected by them even when one has no
personal concern. The Good Samaritan felt pity—and acted
on it. When Victor stopped setting Monsieur Guérin's place
at table, he did not feel pity; he sensed that he had made a
mistake. Partially because he could not easily conceive of
other states of mind outside his own, Victor could not reach a
point of view from which other persons' lives and happiness
had reality and importance for him.

This was the first obstacle to further development. He remained almost totally self-absorbed, as do most of us a large
part of the time. However, we like to think that we can overcome our selfishness in order to feel pity and show charity
toward others, and to act in the name of something larger
than ourselves—country, religion, rule of law, beauty, virtue.
Victor could not begin to erect such complex concepts in his
mind. He was in every way an egotist without loyalty or pity;
and he was our blood brother.

It takes Itard only a page to treat Victor's selfishness. He needs four pages to discuss sex, the second obstacle, whereas he had gotten by with a dozen lines on the subject in the first report. At seventeen, Victor was going through a "pronounced stage of puberty." For three or four years Itard had been expecting a major change, and he hoped that it would release new impulses and aspirations that would "enlarge his moral existence." Sometimes I believe Itard yearned for a second drive in Victor's life to displace or at least compete with eating. But he never says it that way.

I saw this long-awaited puberty arrive, or rather explode. Our young Savage has been consumed by continuous and violent desires without the faintest idea of their object and without showing the slightest preference for any woman. Instead of that expansive spark that usually propels one sex toward the other, I have seen in him only a kind of groping and feeble instinct making him prefer the company of women to that of men. The affections of his heart play no role in this preference. Several times I have watched him in a group of women seek to calm his tenseness by sitting down next to one of them and squeezing her hand, her arms, her knees. Continuing these bizarre caresses, he would feel his unruly desires grow stronger instead of disappear. Then, seeing no way out of his uncomfortable emotions, he would change mood completely. He would push away the woman he had first sought out and go through the same process with another. One day, however, he carried his explorations a little further. After the first caresses, he took the lady by the hand and led her without the slightest violence into an alcove.

There, showing a kind of embarrassment, with an extraordinary expression made up of gaiety and sadness, boldness and uncertainty, he kept holding out his cheek as if to ask the lady to caress him. Then, after walking around her a few times, he finally threw himself on her shoulders and clutched her neck tightly. That was all, and these amorous demonstrations ended, like the others, when he pushed her spitefully away.

It was a pathetic situation. Itard described it as straightforwardly as contemporary taste and official style permitted. Other documents inform us that the scenes were sometimes more tense and embarrassing than Itard implies. One wonders what women participated, and if Itard instructed them how to respond to Victor. Itard had opened this section of his report with a kind of summary statement: "But what seems even more astonishing [than his egotism] in the emotional life of this young man is his indifference toward women while undergoing the obvious effects of a very pronounced puberty crisis." Was anyone responsible for this situation? Should anything be done? Itard was in as much of a quandary as Victor.

In the woods, the Wild Boy probably saw animals mating. But what did he really *see?* His powers of observation and imitation had developed only in the past year or two. What reason would he have to notice animals coupling or to relate their behavior to himself? Instinct? A common word, but what does it mean? In Rodez and in Paris, Victor had probably seen very little of the courtship and mating behavior of men and women. He had virtually no exchanges with the other children who filled the institute; he was not allowed to roam the streets. No one could *tell* him the facts of life. We can only surmise that he had almost nothing to go on.

All considered, Victor approached the problem of discovering what to do about his sexual appetites with considerable resourcefulness and insight. Something must have tipped him off about women. All he needed was a little response or co-operation from his partners, but they held back. A totally sheltered child, brought up away from society and books, and without any information on sex, would probably act the same way. There is nothing astonishing about Victor's touching mixture of curiosity, desire, and frustration. It springs directly from the fact that his training, magnificent as it was, kept him in a prolonged state of social isolation. If he had been encouraged to play and study with the deaf-mutes in the institute, most of whom were normal and full of life, his social and even sexual conduct might have been different. But this was not to be.

Itard and Madame Guérin did the best they could with baths, special diet, and lots of exercise to ease Victor's puberty crisis. He finally stopped his clumsy approaches to women. But sometimes he fell into strange furious moods, shouted and sobbed and tore his clothes. He went so far as to scratch or bite his governess. Then he would be filled with remorse; he wanted to kiss the places he had injured. He began to have nosebleeds. Itard found he could calm the boy by bleeding him, but the cure did not last long.

Using all his medical and psychological experience, Itard made little progress toward reducing Victor's turbulence. It threatened now to interrupt the whole program of reeducation. Could the young doctor do more? It was a double impasse. On the one hand, how much responsibility could Itard take as guardian and foster father to instruct Victor in the facts of sex? On the other hand, was there any reason to believe that such instruction would relieve Victor's problem rather than aggravate it? Itard faces this double dilemma in the last paragraph of his report, before the brief conclusion. His answer is eloquent and honest. Notice that he speaks of "instinct" in Victor; under normal circumstances, Itard would have rejected the word in reference to human beings. He also uses the traditional distinction between physical need of the senses and love for the other sex residing in the "heart." Some might say Itard lacked the courage to see his experiment all the way through. I would say that he had the courage to remain firm in observing the difference between a scientific experiment of reeducation and tampering with the life of another human being. Here is the whole last paragraph, the symmetrical counterpart of the paragraph that closes his first report on the same subject (see page 117).

Such was the critical period of puberty that had promised so much. It would probably have fulfilled our hopes if, instead of concentrating all its force on his senses, it had affected his whole character and sense of being [*système moral*] and had lighted in his heart the passion of love. Nevertheless, having thought things over very deeply, I shall not hide the fact that I was mistaken to expect puberty to develop that way in Victor. I should never have thought of him as an ordinary adolescent, one in whom the love of women precedes, or at least accompanies, sexual maturity. This harmony between our needs and our inclinations could not develop in a being who had never learned the difference between a man and a woman. He could rely only on instinct to give him a glimpse of this difference, without even relating it to the present situation. I had no doubt that if we had cared to reveal to this young man the secret of his anxieties and the goal of his desires, we would have gained an incalculable advantage. On the other hand, supposing I had the authority to try this experiment, didn't I have to fear that I would be revealing to our young Savage a need that he would satisfy as publicly as his other needs and that it would lead him to acts of a revolting indecency? I had to hold back, intimidated by

fear of such an outcome. I resigned myself, as many
times before, to watching my hopes fade away before an
unforeseen obstacle.

The other times, however, he had not resigned himself and
had found a way around the obstacle. This time he stopped
short, accepting the barriers we call decorum, privacy, taboo.
I believe we should respect his decision. The narrative part of
the second report ends on that sad, slightly bitter, worldly-
wise note. Itard was all of thirty-two; Victor was about seventeen. They had worked together for over five years. Now the
teacher felt it was useless to continue a course of instruction
that had transformed a savage into a half-civilized young man.

The Second Report

The year 1805 was crucial both for Victor and for Itard.
The doctor stopped the training sessions and turned the boy
over to Madame Guérin. Her official responsibility was re-
affirmed in a letter sent in May 1806 by the Minister of the
Interior to the Institute for Deaf-Mutes ordering continua-
tion of the 150-franc yearly salary "for her trouble and care"
as guardian of the Savage of Aveyron. From this moment on,
Victor slips into obscurity. What we know about the rest of
his life does not take long to tell.

In 1810, Sicard and three administrators at the institute
wrote to the Minister of the Interior that all hopes of civiliz-
ing the boy had disappeared. Sicard reverted to his original
diagnosis of "complete idiocy." The letter stated the boy's
presence at the institute created disciplinary problems with
the other students. They were particularly distressed that
Madame Guérin's continued residence and frequent visits

from her daughters introduced females into an institution that had become all male. Victor was no longer wanted. The minister granted their request that Madame Guérin be paid 500 francs for expenses in addition to her salary so that she could take the boy somewhere else to live. It was stipulated that "Dr. Itard will not lose sight of him." In 1811, after eleven years inside the institute, Madame Guérin and Victor moved into a house around the corner on a tiny street called the Impasse des Feuillantines. They lived there for the next seventeen years. Our only information on those years is negative: the boy, who was now a man, caused no recorded incident, complaint, or scandal. As a boy just entering his teens, Victor Hugo lived only four houses away for two years. It is possible that the occasional references in his novels and poems to a "fabulous monster" refer obliquely to the younger Victor's hearing stories about the Wild Boy of Aveyron—or perhaps to encountering him in the streets and back alleys around the institute. Some witnesses said that until the end he was recognizable by his cumbersome gait. Yet the once notorious Wild Boy now became an unnoticed feature in the landscape. In 1828, at approximately forty, he died. No official documents or published notices have been found to establish the cause of death or to state where he is buried. We do not even know whether his last years were happy, or at least peaceful. He was a forgotten man, as Itard had already said twenty years before. He was no longer referred to as Victor after Itard disappeared from his life, simply as the Savage. Forty is not a ripe old age. But it is old enough to tell us that Victor did not pine away for the woods of his boyhood; he found some way of making a life for himself in that dead-end street on the outskirts of Paris. Being mute, he could never tell his own story.

By an irony of timing and circumstance, however, the story

of the Wild Boy's training became available in print just at the moment that he disappeared from view as a newsworthy figure. A month after the letter renewing Madame Guérin's salary in 1806, a new Minister of the Interior, Champagny, wrote to Itard asking him "in the name of humanity and science" to write a detailed report on the education he had given Victor. In September, Itard sent in a fifty-page report and enclosed a copy of his earlier account of the first nine months, published in 1801 by the Society of Observers of Man. The minister passed the documents on for evaluation to the French Academy, where they were read by the Committee on History and Ancient Literature. That committee included philosophers and investigators we would today call social scientists. A month later they responded, heaping praise on Itard's work and attributing the limited results not to his methods but to the boy's condition. In a further letter the minister told Itard that the institute "recognizes that you could not have put into your lessons, exercises, and experiments any more intelligence, wisdom, patience, and courage than you did." The minister decided to print the report at government expense and to supply Itard with all the copies he wanted. "In order to secure the full development of Victor's faculties, I ask you to continue the efforts that have already produced such favorable results and to determine whether the time has not come to teach him a mechanical trade."

Itard did not continue his efforts, nor apparently did Victor learn a trade. Yet the minister granted everything Itard could have hoped for—recognition and praise for himself, official publication of his report, and adequate financial support for the boy and his guardian. But the training program had come to a standstill more than a year earlier. It is not hard to imagine Itard's discouragement and mental fatigue after five years of exhausting daily routine. He needed relief; he may well have thought Victor did also.

At the same time, Itard had his professional career to attend to. During the work with Victor he had completed and successfully defended his medical thesis on pneumothorax, a lung condition. The 500-franc yearly stipend he had received for training Victor did not go very far. As health officer for the institute he received only 66 francs a year in addition to his rooms. He was still a poor man, though no longer unknown. In the next few years he did well enough in his private practice to rent an office-apartment in central Paris where patients could consult him more easily. He continued to spend much of his time at the institute. About 1805, he began to train students with some residual hearing by using methods he had developed for Victor. Three years later he published the first of a series of articles demonstrating that some deaf-mutes could be taught to hear and understand spoken sentences, and even to speak. This restless researcher could not confine himself forever to one case history.

Basically, Itard stopped working with Victor because he thought no more could be accomplished. The difference in tone and presentation between his two reports reveals a great deal about how Itard had changed in five years. The opening section of the first report refers to his "successes" in training the young Savage, and the document closes with five ringing affirmations about the universal nature of man in the light of his exceptional experiment. The 1806 report does without the high-flown style. This time Itard generally shuns philosophy and theory and lets the facts of the case speak for themselves in fifty-six short, numbered sections. Five years of working and thinking had reduced his claims to universal knowledge and increased his wisdom.

But something very subtle happens beneath the muted

style of the second report. Unprodded, Itard would probably not have written up the case again. He was ready to forget what he considered to be the record of his failure. Obliged by the minister to go over his notes and evaluate the entire course of training, he began to modify his outlook. At the close of the report, he drew up a careful balance sheet. The facts presented lead to "uncertainty" and "basic conflict" about how to evaluate the results. On the one hand, seven key sections of the report (he cites them by number) imply three negative conclusions:

1. Because he cannot hear the speech of others and learn to speak himself, Victor's education is and will remain incomplete.
2. His "intellectual" progress will never match that of children normally brought up in society.
3. His emotional development is blocked by profound egotism and by the impossibility of channeling his awakening sexual feelings toward any satisfactory goals.

On the other hand, twenty-one sections show things in a more favorable light and justify four positive conclusions:

1. The training of Victor's sight and touch has enlarged his perception of the world and "powerfully contributed to the development of his intellectual faculties."
2. Learning written signs and using them to communicate with people around him represents a remarkable achievement.
3. Despite the indelible streak of wildness in him, Victor has shown himself capable of fond friendship, the desire to please by good behavior, and sincere remorse over bad behavior.

4. No matter how one interprets the various facts in the second report, "everything recommends this extraordinary young man to the attention of scientists, to the solicitude of those who care for him, and to the protection of the government."

These are the closing words of the report. It would be difficult to draw conclusions more even-handedly than Itard did about his own work.

The opening pages of the report, however, show a more significant shift in perspective.

> Your Excellency . . . without the formal order from you to draft a report, I would have buried my undertaking in silence and oblivion. Its final result offers less the story of the pupil's progress than the story of the teacher's failure. But . . . to appreciate the present state of the Savage of Aveyron, one should recall his past condition. To be judged properly, this young man can be compared only to himself.

Itard's "but" introduces a major new consideration: against what should one measure Victor's progress? In the first report, Itard stated that when he began to work with Victor the boy had reached the mental age of an infant of ten to twelve months and responded rapidly to socialization and training. This description probably appeared accurate for a year or so. But four more years made Itard change his mind about the base line. He refers to "that animal-man," and then goes on to make an even more severe appraisal of where Victor started from.

> Such was the state of this boy's physical and moral faculties that he ranked not only among the lowest of his species but even among the lowest animals. One could

go so far as to say that he differed from a plant only because he could move and make sounds. Between this sub-animal and Victor's present condition there is an enormous distance.

This new assessment of the five-year training program virtually transforms failure into success. Don't compare Victor to a boy of his own age. Remember what he was like at the start and how far he has come since then. He was almost a *plant*; now he is almost a *man*.

In the end, writing the report made the difference. As he described the training that became increasingly discouraging at the time, Itard rediscovered faith in himself and in Victor. Their long work together had not been time wasted, for Victor had begun from a far lower level of development, or of deprivation, than anyone realized. Itard was no longer ashamed of his "failure." The straightforward prose of the second report cannot always conceal his wonder at his own accomplishment, and that of Victor and Madame Guérin. The explanation is simple. Often we do not grasp what has happened to us until we tell someone else about it. Odysseus, when asked to recount his life, was sometimes moved to weep over his own story as he told it. Itard's two reports, especially the second, record and preserve a story he did not understand fully until he wrote it down for the Minister of the Interior, and for himself, and for us.

5

Wildness, Greatness, and Desire

Master and Pupil

After he came out of the woods, the Wild Boy fell into the hands of a succession of remarkable people. Right away, Constans-Saint-Estève, the commissioner in Saint-Sernin, grasped the significance of the case. Bonnaterre and Itard watched him closely for six months and five years respectively, and we remember them today for the reliable accounts they wrote of their observations. Two other people, both of them uneducated and of lowly origins, played essential roles in the story without attaining any fame. Clair, the gardener at the Central School in Rodez, treated his charge like a human child even though he acted like a wild animal. According to all accounts, Madame Guérin had the gift of com-

162

bining love with firmness. The boy's "savage" behavior did not unnerve the steady humanity of his two keepers. For him they represented both family and society. To us they look like the salt of the earth.

We know more about Itard, principally from his own writings. He went on to become a famous doctor and an enlightened educator, one of the first to understand that the deaf should be trained not only to sign but also to read and write. But he never surpassed the insight and persuasive power of the two texts on the Wild Boy. It would be hard to say which was stronger in him, detached scientific and philosophical interest in the nature of man in general, or affection and concern for his pupil Victor. His reserve of patience seemed limitless. He had a talent for designing progressive exercises to lead gradually around mental or psychological roadblocks. When Victor couldn't perceive marks on paper as anything remotely connected with what we call writing, Itard went all the way back to cardboard cutouts of simple shapes and worked up slowly to metal letters, then words, then meanings. It took the better part of a year. A mere pedagogue would have given up in a few months or even weeks.

Itard seemed to know by instinct how to fade out cues in order to sharpen the boy's responses. He was determined to design his training to fit the individual case, and he rejected from the start the "ordinary method of social education." It sounds elementary to develop "special education" to fit a special case, but that approach was not practiced even in the Institute for Deaf-Mutes, where all pupils received the same treatment. Itard also followed a carefully thought-out order of events. He tried to make Victor feel at home in his new environment and to awaken his simplest sense perceptions before going on to train his higher intellectual and affective faculties.

It is the last two aspects of Itard's program that most impressed and inspired two influential modern educators. Edouard Seguin worked with Itard for a year at the end of the older man's life, to train a deeply retarded boy, probably an idiot. Having benefited from Itard's skill and dedication, Seguin went on in 1839 to found the first school in France for the mentally retarded. Forced to emigrate to the United States in 1851 for political reasons, Seguin became one of the founding fathers of special education for the mentally deficient in Massachusetts, Pennsylvania, and New York. Maria Montessori, an Italian psychiatrist at the turn of the century, recognized the importance of Seguin's work and devoted herself to pre-school education for normal children. Both she and Seguin acknowledged their lasting debt to Itard's approach and technique in working with Victor, particularly his willingness to begin by training the senses and motor skills. The metal cutouts Itard made to teach Victor to recognize shapes and letters are used today all over the world in special education classes and in Montessori schools.

While he worked to direct the boy's development, Itard observed everything. Here lay the source of his strength. His two reports record the steadiness of his gaze and his constant effort to interpret what he saw without mistaking performance or behavior for comprehension on the boy's part.

However, a troubling reservation underlies the admiration for Itard's work felt by a large number of educators and psychologists. Many of them believe that the amazing feat of training the Wild Boy would never have occurred had it not been for the initial error of Itard's diagnosis. Convinced in his own mind that the boy was "all there," Itard, according to this view, rehabilitated an idiot and thus proved it could be done. In an official speech honoring Itard after his death, a doctor named Bousquet stated the position concisely. "To reeducate a child whose faculties have merely gone to sleep is not much more than an ordinary education. But to train an idiot, to turn a disgusting antisocial creature into a bearable obedient boy—this is a victory over nature, it is almost a new creation." The full measure of Itard's accomplishment, then, would rest on the faultiness of his diagnosis of the Wild Boy's condition and his rejection of Pinel's "correct" diagnosis. Those who praise Itard most for his humaneness and his success as an educator reject the very foundation on which he based his program: the boy's basic organic health and the functional or social origins of his condition. They believe he trained a true idiot to adapt to society beyond all previous expectations; he believed he had trained a boy whose isolation from society had made him *act* like an idiot.

There is a certain irony in the belief that Itard succeeded as an educator because he failed as a diagnostician. Yet Seguin, the champion and redeemer of the mentally retarded, based his career on this premise.

In any case, we must assess the weaknesses of Itard's training program along with its strengths. To begin with, Itard limited Victor's social environment very severely. Even though the boy lived at the Institute for Deaf-Mutes, where Itard was resident physician, he apparently was not encouraged to play with boys and girls of his age—even of his mental age. Madame Guérin took him on regular walks. He sawed a little firewood. He got soft and fat. The assumption that he was already well coordinated physically cut him off from a number of group activities that might have developed his capacities for self-control, imitation, and competition. Itard's pedagogy was brilliant yet somewhat rigid, and he left little opportunity for Victor to learn for himself through free activity. By spoon-feeding him, Itard almost placed the Wild Boy in a new, looser form of isolation. The root cause of his backwardness was not completely removed. Like a little prince, Victor had a tutor and a governess, whereas what he probably needed most was to work and play with other children. It might have been impossible to overcome his fears, but Itard records no attempt to encourage him in that direction.

The second drawback of Itard's program is the excessive stress he laid on training Victor to speak. Itard believed that only by talking would the boy integrate himself into society and, perhaps, reveal the secrets of his past. That obsession led to certain mistakes. Itard failed to encourage the speech sounds Victor produced spontaneously—*oh, lli* (for Julie), Madame Guérin's exclamation *Oh Dieu*, and a few more. They seemed too unfocused and clumsy. But psychologists have discovered in similar cases that results can be obtained by reinforcing any and all speech sounds and refining them later, a technique Itard applied in some of his other exercises. The program of vowel recognition Itard attempted early in 1802 was probably too difficult for Victor's untrained ear. In 1805, after failing to teach the boy vocal articulation after a year's work starting with elementary mimicry, Itard seems to have given up on language. At this point he "abandoned" Victor to "incurable muteness." Apparently he did not consider going back a third time to reading and writing, skills the boy had almost achieved and by which several celebrated deaf-mutes had developed their intelligence and made their careers. Itard wanted *vocal* speech at all costs and would accept no substitute.

As a result, he overlooked or decided against several avenues of training. Most obviously, in that particular institution, Itard never tried to find out if Victor could learn to sign, to use the language that was being used all around him and for which he had a natural propensity. For he already used an "action language" of his own. There was a deep prejudice at work in Itard, one he recognized and reversed at the end of his life. Sign was the language of the "dumb"— an association Itard wanted to avoid. Itard thought it necessary to shield Victor from the competing temptation of this inferior language. During all his forty years at the Institute, Itard never learned to sign. He acknowledged later that signing stimulates the mind and expresses ideas as effectively as vocal speech. It is hard not to believe that the Wild Boy's story would have followed a different course if he had been taught to sign.

I must also find fault with Itard for not having made a new attempt to trace the boy's origins while the trail around Lacaune and Saint-Sernin was still somewhat warm. Guiraud had carried out an investigation without finding the boy's parents. The whole situation might have been different if Itard had directed some of his energy and imagination into pursuing the clues and rumors that surrounded the boy's infant years. But the teacher in Itard made stronger claims on him than the scientific investigator.

My last criticism of Itard, like the previous two, points less at what he did than at what he failed to do. He made few plans about Victor's emotional training after the boy was partly socialized. More thought on the subject might have led Itard to realize that the boy would have trouble understanding puberty without friends of his own age. All one can really say is that Itard seems not to have anticipated the emotional and sexual problems that Victor faced during the crucial months of his training. There was a plan for everything else; here nature was expected to take its course. In the artificial environment Itard had constructed around the boy, nature had no course to take. The result was frustration and resistance.

Itard performed and recorded a stunning feat in rehabilitating the Wild Boy. The hard fact remains, however, that after the display of so much resourcefulness and human affection by Madame Guérin and Itard, the boy did not come all the way back to "normal" human capacities and responses. Were Itard's methods at fault? Probably not, or not completely. Was it just too late to reeducate the boy? Probably so, as Itard himself suggests many times, particularly at the close of his first report, in discussing Victor's inadequate "faculty of imitation." (I shall consider this "critical age" hypothesis in Appendix II in connection with the case of Genie.) Itard was concerned primarily with speech, of course, as are many modern theorists on developmental psychology. There seems to be good justification, looking at Victor's whole story, to extend those notions of timing and development to the process of ego-formation. We could well say that it was just too late for Victor to assemble, become conscious of, and enact an idea of his *self*, of his identity as a separate person. The imagery of sleep that surrounds the Wild Boy stands for the incompleteness of his self-awareness; he never fully awoke to his individual existence.

Or was the Wild Boy an idiot after all, as Pinel's committee had first reported to the Society of Observers of Man? At first, this theory appears to solve many problems in the case. Idiocy provides a potential motive for the boy's original abandonment in the forest. It would explain his limited progress in language. Having never learned to speak in the first place, an idiot would have no language to forget and therefore be mute when captured. A great number of intelligent scientists have accepted this theory, from the psychiatrist Esquirol, one of Pinel's students and a contemporary of Itard, to Lévi-Strauss, the modern ethnographer. The difficulty is that most of these men tend to take the position that all abandoned children are idiots. A look into a few foundling homes seriously weakens that extreme view.

Several other factors undermine the idiocy theory. Could a genuine idiot, lacking coordination and the ability to plan and to care for himself, survive alone in the woods? It is very doubtful—unless the period of abandonment was fairly short. But the most reliable accounts place the boy in the woods utterly on his own for at least three years, and for as many as six. Idiocy would also seem to exclude the kind of striking improvement Victor made during the first nine months under Itard, and even his later, slower advances. Twice, in the second report, Itard uses the word "spontaneously" to describe the boy's actions. The first applies to his exploratory use of cutout letters to designate the objects around him, the second to qualify his "new way of seeing things" after discovering that he could combine unrelated objects to make a chalk-holder. He learned to concentrate and to apply himself. He developed a rudimentary curiosity and inventiveness. From the time of his capture, the boy was particular about what he ate, a characteristic idiots do not usually show. The idiocy theory presents serious drawbacks that are hard to dismiss.

Two other hypotheses have a greater claim to serious attention. One is that the Wild Boy, though born normal, developed a serious mental or psychological disturbance *before* his abandonment. Precocious schizophrenia, infantile psychosis, autism—a number of technical terms have been applied to his condition. Several psychiatrists I have consulted favor this approach. It provides both a motivation for abandonment and an explanation for his partial recovery under Itard's treatment. Mental or psychological disturbance does not make survival in the woods so unlikely as the idiocy theory does.

The third approach is of course Itard's thesis, boldly proclaimed in his first report and still present, though muted, in the second. He differed categorically with Pinel about both the "cause and the curability" of the boy's condition. Early in the first report, Itard affirms that "seven years of isolation" from all human society are enough to explain the boy's physical and mental state. Itard further believed that such a condition caused by the environment should be reversible, curable under proper care in an improved environment. On that basis, he set to work.

After pondering the claims of these three theories for several years in the light of the evidence, I can only state that none is either proven or disproven. I believe that idiocy is the weakest. Of the latter two, one cannot summarily dismiss Itard's position. It is indirectly supported by a few documented cases in this century. Normal children under six or eight shut in by their parents often come out of two to four years of total confinement in worse condition than the Wild Boy. Often they cannot walk or feed themselves. They are invariably mute and indifferent to their surroundings. Genie is such a case (see Appendix II). Yet correlations between cases are hard to make. We shall probably never discover what the Wild Boy was subjected to before his abandonment.

Another reason for considering Itard's theory is simply that the man closest to the boy believed it and wagered a large part of his career on demonstrating it. However, an unexpected difficulty crops up here. Itard apparently changed his mind, at least in part. He modified his position slightly when, in his second report, he qualified what he had said in 1801 about the Wild Boy's curability. In 1806 he kept insisting that certain malfunctions in the boy's constitution—principally in his speech centers and in his ability to imitate—were irreversible. It was simply too late to do anything about it. The mechanisms were permanently atrophied.

Then, many years later, in the paper written in 1828 on treating mutism in the mentally deficient, Itard made a further statement. He was describing how careful a doctor must be to determine that a partially retarded patient has capacities adequate to justify lengthy and tedious speech training. He cautions that lively and apparently intelligent participation in games and exercises is not enough unless the pupil can generalize what he learns to the rest of his behavior. And then Itard adds this sobering sentence: "It is because I was once mistaken on this score myself that I add this remark." Almost certainly he is referring to Victor, who had just died without making a ripple. Itard is not recanting his original claim that isolation alone was enough to cause the boy's lamentable condition. But he is reversing himself on the wisdom of trying for five years to restore him to normal speech, intelligence, and social behavior. He had been too optimistic, too ambitious. This is a fifty-year-old doctor looking back at his enthusiasm at twenty-five and shaking his head wisely and sadly.

Gineste, the psychiatrist who has cautioned against any firm diagnosis, redirects our attention toward the circumstances that enabled Itard—a twenty-five-year-old medical student in 1800—to see a potentially complete human being where everyone else saw a hopeless idiot fit to be cast out of human society. Gineste has probed deep into the medical, moral, pedagogical, and unconscious attachments that affected the master in dealing with his pupil. Almost surely Itard's early successes, and perhaps his later difficulties, are attributable to the countertransference which linked him strongly and personally to his patient. In any case, Gineste finds it significant that Itard was not a regular practitioner of what we now call psychiatry; fresh insights into the boy's mode of being, some of them unsystematic and subjective, prompted his involvement in the case and took the place of a professional diagnosis.

Behind Those Restless Eyes

Four men set down reliable firsthand accounts of the Wild
Boy of Aveyron, each account longer, more probing, and
more purposeful than the last: Constans's early report, Bonnaterre's pamphlet, Virey's fifty-page supplement to his book,
and Itard's two reports. All four men were looking for a child
of nature, basically a philosophical idea. All four, when they
saw the boy, responded to an individual human being. As
they watched his movements and the unhidden play of feelings across his face, they asked themselves the inevitable questions. What is going on in this boy's mind? What objects does
he perceive? Does he see *me?* What is his sense of the world
outside and of himself in it?

For, in the end, we all yearn to see through eyes other than
our own, to enter another life. Proust called this dream the
"fountain of youth."

The Wild Boy's bestial behavior implied that his mind
worked in ways totally unfamiliar to socialized people. Those
most interested in his case reacted very differently to this
possibility. Virey observed the boy for long periods without
interference and set down everything he saw. Itard, on the
other hand, aimed single-mindedly at retraining the boy in
order to prove a hypothesis about how he had become savage.
But even Itard the activist felt the fascination of the boy's
mere presence. One of the earliest descriptions in Itard's first
report suggests that the boy was not aware of being watched.

It is worth noting that sometimes his mood seemed to
produce a calm expression of regret and melancholy—
a risky conjecture, yet unavoidable if one observed him

carefully. For example, when bad weather drove everyone out of the garden was just the time he chose to go
out. He would walk around for a while and finally sit
down on the edge of the pond.

For hours on end and with indescribable pleasure,
I often stopped everything in order to examine him in
this situation, to see how all his spasmodic movements
and rocking subsided and gave way to more tranquil
behavior. Almost imperceptibly, his vacant or distorted
face took on a pronounced expression of sadness or
revery. Meanwhile, he would stare fixedly at the surface
of the pond and from time to time he would toss onto
it a handful of dried leaves.

Itard wanted to penetrate that inaccessible mind. I suspect he
hoped to solve part of the mystery by teaching the boy to
talk. Then Victor could speak for himself. Yet perplexing
questions arise. Could he use our words for his thoughts?
Wouldn't education and speech change him into something
no longer wild, no longer mysterious? Itard was more than
intelligent enough to grasp these paradoxes, yet he never
mentions them. And he did not suspend his training program.

The firsthand accounts suggest that the Wild Boy passed
through three identifiable stages, and stopped in the middle
of a fourth.

During his years in the woods the boy lost his human culture, his capacity to live in society, and even his memory of
that life. At age ten he must have been a thin, constantly
hungry creature whose life was occupied by one major activity: foraging. He became swift and resourceful in his movements and resistant to hardships like cold and damp. He survived through direct response to his needs—food and sleep
—and a sense of dangers to avoid—falling, predators, poison-

ous foods. His later behavior gives reason to believe that a few exceptional events penetrated this basic texture, as happens also with some animals. A high wind or a full moon or a snowfall could overwhelm his mood and produce a heightened state of mind linked to those sights and sounds. To drink water calmed him and encouraged some rudimentary form of reflection or meditation. Remembered sensations and images were adequate to organize his knowledge about the environment without words, probably without clear ideas. He sniffed his food carefully and, like a monkey, filled vacant moments of wakefulness with rocking. In some fashion he may have perceived trees and berries and streams more sharply than we do, but without the capacity for detachment and association we cultivate. But we can only conjecture about what was really going on in his mind.

I cannot imagine his life as anything but full, constantly active in the need to survive, unthinking yet purposeful. The meaning of his life was to stay alive, and he lived that meaning without being aware of it in any sense we conceive of when we use words. Except during the last year or so, when he occasionally stole or accepted food from the peasants, the boy had reverted very close to the condition of an animal. Still, he had not become hairy, as some fanciful accounts stated, nor did he run on all fours or live in the trees.

And then he was captured. The shock must have been as harsh and as sudden as the previous traumas of abandonment and isolation. His existence in the woods had been full and active, and in its own way well adjusted to the milieu. Now, overnight, his life was emptied of all activity, all purpose, all meaning. The creature that had run wild was confined to a room or a walled garden and walked like a dog on a leash. His basic needs were supplied, and instead of having to forage he was expected to wear clothes, eat strange foods, sleep in a bed, and control his natural functions. During nine months in Rodez and Paris, first cared for and then shamefully neglected, the boy displayed many different behaviors. Yet a kind of pattern is visible. He retreated into a deep apathy toward everything not related to eating or escaping. He did not even perceive the rest of his surroundings. People did not interest him. Rocking filled hours of his time. He became fat and gave the impression of stupidity. Yet the tiniest sight or sound associated with eating or escaping galvanized him into swift accurate motion. Dullness turned instantly into shrewd activity. Bonnaterre describes how a guest cut a morsel from meat on his plate and offered it to the boy. He accepted the morsel and then, in a flash, filched the whole slice. Bonnaterre and Virey agree that at this stage those bursts of purposeful behavior were totally selfish. He served his own appetites and displayed no feeling toward people who fed or petted him. When tickled, he laughed easily; Nougairoles and Virey speak of his having a lovely laugh. Aristotle and St. Augustine believed that recognizably human life begins in the early months when an infant smiles, for he smiles at his mother, responding to her coaxing and caresses. There is no record in this period of early captivity that Victor smiled, let alone smiled at anyone. Bonnaterre had to find consolation in the fact that the boy grew taller and finally caught his first cold! When Itard took charge of him, the boy had sunk into deep lethargy and foulness, with moments of biting and scratching.

Three or four months later, during a third period that lasted probably two or three years, Itard was dealing with a person so responsive, so close to full humanity that Itard gave him a name. Within limits, Victor could pay attention, understand and follow verbal instructions, play games, care for himself, and even make spontaneous inventions using familiar objects. His progress and the very expression on his face encouraged Madame Guérin and Itard to treat him as a full human being who would overcome the severe handicap of his years in the woods. Itard welcomed moments of emotional excitement in Victor—anger, tears of frustration or relief, outbursts of affection—for they appeared to be "salutary crises" that would bring the boy closer to human sentiment, as a storm may clear the atmosphere. At least Victor had strong responses.

His inner thoughts remain shrouded, of course. He wore clothes and used his own chamber pot; but Itard's comments imply that Victor, in spite of his training, developed no sense of shame or modesty. Several unverifiable stories circulated about his occasional immodest behavior in public. How did he perceive himself among the people around him? We are tempted to say he "loved" Madame Guérin and Itard, yet he continued to avoid other people, especially those his own age, to prefer solitude to company, and to escape when the opportunity offered itself. The old "wild" reactions to wind and moon and snow never disappeared, as if they represented a profound layer of identity that no training could efface. There was always something incomplete and precarious about Victor's domestication. Turned loose, he would probably have reverted to his former ways; his place in society was artificial and had to be maintained by a guardian. He was probably more a prisoner than a pensioner. Still, he had used words spontaneously, he had shown selective affection for those who protected him, and he had a sense of expected behavior and reward that Itard called justice. This must be a human creature.

After Itard's second report, the Wild Boy lived on for twenty-two years with Madame Guérin, most of them in a little house near the Institute for Deaf-Mutes. The experiment of retraining was over, and Itard turned to other medical and educational projects. No one bothered to follow the boy's progress any longer. This fourth period represents a partial relapse. In 1816, when the "Savage," as he was still called, was approaching thirty, Virey wrote a lengthy encyclopedia article on "wild men." He conscientiously went back to check on the only case he had observed firsthand, sixteen years earlier. After a two-page summary of the boy's history, Virey dismissed the final years of the boy's life in one harsh sentence: "Today this individual remains fearful [*effaré*], half wild, incapable of learning to speak in spite of all attempts to teach him." We can surmise that the boy had formed no further links to individuals or the community. Whatever sexual drives he felt had diminished without ever focusing on women as a possible source of gratification. After a fashion, his life was probably full again—full of the familiar persons, places, and actions of an existence built on routine. A state pension kept him alive, like an animal in the zoo, and when he died no one noticed. For a few years, lifted by the strong arms of a dedicated teacher, his faculties had emerged from the stifling layers of lethargy and animality. But they fell back again into listlessness as soon as he was left to his own devices. He did not have the enterprise or the imagination to challenge himself to be other than what he was.

Can we approach any closer to the boy's mind than this analysis into four periods of uneven development? Only, I believe, if we accept the imaginative leap that poets and novelists rely on to create their characters. Accordingly, I shall quote from a work whose portrayal of an exceptional state of awareness in a youth will lead us further toward the Wild Boy's elusive consciousness.

The English romantic poet Wordsworth describes how a boy he knew, who died young, sometimes perceived landscape as a total vision of forms, colors, and sounds—as an undivided presence. This Boy of Winander was able to communicate directly with nature as an embodied spirit. To behold the scene in its entirety was a complete act needing no words or gestures, just as the "steady lake" in his poem seems to "receive" through deep communion the scene that surrounds it.

"There was a boy . . ." the poem begins. He loves walking alone in the hills of Winander at evening. Through his clasped hands he can blow a hooting sound that the owls often answer from all around the lake. But sometimes they remain quiet, and in the mounting silence, something transpires that links the boy to the watching lake, to waiting nature, to everything.

> . . . and, when a lengthened pause
> Of silence came and baffled his best skill,
> Then sometimes, in that silence while he hung
> Listening, a gentle shock of mild surprise
> Has carried far into his heart the voice
> Of mountain torrents; or the visible scene
> Would enter unawares into his mind,
> With all its solemn imagery, its rocks,
> Its woods, and that uncertain heaven, received
> Into the bosom of the steady lake.

When he described the Wild Boy sitting by the pond at the institute, Itard was trying to evoke a similar mood. Was something comparable going on in Victor's sensibility when he went to the window to drink his precious water and look out at the garden and the trees? Like Itard, we would be hard put to say whether those moments represented a kind of atavism, a reversion to primitive perceptions and feelings, or a heightened form of communion known to deeply reflective minds like Wordsworth's. In a sobering sentence Rousseau wrote, "Man, a being who meditates, is a depraved animal." It is those moments of "depravity" that fascinate us in the Wild Boy and seem to bring him close to human consciousness. But they remain solitary, and uncommunicated, the movements of a very rudimentary ego we cannot penetrate.

Our Deepest Desires

The story of the Wild Boy of Aveyron haunts our collective memory for reasons that deserve attention even though they may be difficult to express. I believe I can approach them best in a roundabout way.

What do we most deeply desire? If we found Aladdin's lamp and a genie to do our bidding, what would we make of our lives? We tend to smile or shrug at such basic questions. For we are constantly tempted by things we think we want and later find we don't. To live like a king, or like a rich celebrity, with the world at our feet—is this the height of bliss? Our imaginations whisper to us about a land of milk and honey, a paradise of love and eternal youth. It may be impossible to know what we want most.

But there are ways to glimpse the innermost yearnings of mankind. In three places at least, people leave a record of their desires: in myths, in art, and in dreams. These areas lie very close together, and all three seem to tell us that at the deepest level we desire not one big thing—like happiness or love, power or knowledge—but a few interwoven and often contradictory things. The great stories, from Adam and Eve to *Faust* and *Madame Bovary*, and all remembered history, give us insight into those few desires.

We wish to seize what is there before us, to master what we

see, to leave our mark on the world by subduing and appro-
priating it. We also wish to confer life on what lies around us,
to give it form and vigor. Carried to this full extent, those are
the desires to destroy and to create. In most forms of action,
both desires are at work. It happens that way in the exercise
of power, in the accumulation of wealth, in the elaborate
rituals of sex and love. Few people's lives are so simple as to
be ruled by only one desire. Conflict defines us. To live at all
means to be under stress. It is only natural, then, that conflict
should produce in us very early an intermittent yet powerful
longing to escape from our lives.

Escape embraces two different directions or movements.
Children in daydreams and adults in their myths and in their
deeds reveal a profound wish to fly. Icarus' melted wings,
Leonardo's drawings, and legions of angels and wingèd
creatures proclaim our yearning to rise above our lot and
glide far away. If we could fly, we would achieve ubiquity
and omniscience, almost a form of salvation lifting us above
worldly cares to a higher existence. The bird that soars and
swoops overhead can go anywhere. We imagine him happy.
"Free as a bird," the saying goes. We dream of wings because
they would bring magic transcendence.

The other form of escape looks less attractive at first
glance. But I believe that it has even wider appeal. At times
we wish to withdraw into a hole, into ourselves, like turtles.
We retreat not just from hardship and pain but from the
simple responsibility of getting up every day to face the
world as ourselves. How can we go on when other people
expect so much from us? We begin to shrink from our own
fragile identities, from family and friends, from the whole
culture that surrounds us like an attentive audience whenever we venture forth. At such moments, any return to an
earlier and simpler life attracts us, especially the kind of exis-

tence we believe animals have. "I believe I could turn and live with animals," Walt Whitman wrote, "they are so placid and self-contain'd." Claude Lévi-Strauss ends his highly sophisticated book about the difficulties of studying human cultures with a long, wistful sentence about "relaxing our grip" in order to glimpse human nature as it was before thought and before culture "in the glance of understanding . . . we can sometimes exchange with a cat."

A similar atavism lurks in many of our myths. Ovid's *Metamorphoses* collects stories of perplexed and wounded people whose final consolation is to be changed into plants and animals. They have earned their peace. Rip Van Winkle represents the slumber of unconcern into which, at some time, we have all longed to lapse. Folk tales and fairy stories never stray far from the world of animals. Instead of carrying us to a higher existence, this form of escape cradles us in a lower state of being. How wonderful to become an animal free of the burdens men have heaped upon themselves!

It is here that the Wild Boy of Aveyron enters our imaginations. "The whole country of France," we are told, was enthralled by stories of this being as soon as he was discovered. One of the great medical practitioners of the era gave the better part of five years of his life to observing and training the boy. The case has absorbed psychologists and educators, linguists and film directors. The attraction of those people for the case springs, I believe, from a simple perception. The Wild Boy had escaped from humanity into animality; yet it seemed possible that he could be brought back to inform us about the gap in nature he had crossed. No one ever proposed that the boy possessed a special gift or pointed the way toward a superior life. He was no god or idol. People turned out to gape at him because, though alive and biologically functioning, the boy had sunk into a great forgetfulness that dulls the pangs of mortality. In the scores of articles the boy inspired, his contemporaries talked frequently about "waking this creature from his sleep." And so they did—up to a point. Yet one also senses that many people were drawn to his unthinking existence as if they, too, yearned to lay aside their everyday identities and responsibilities. Their pity shades into envy. We can easily feel the tug of this response. The Wild Boy appears to have been utterly unconcerned with power and status, with ego and sex. That eerie moral weightlessness in his story evokes dreams and yearnings familiar to us all.

The Wild Boy's story does not solve the problems of human nature and human culture, but it obliges us to reflect on how to live with those unsolved questions. It demonstrates the power and vividness of an individual case history compared to generalizations based on statistically valid samples. A careful case study, like Itard's two reports, avoids rash claims about discovering the truth* and maintains a healthy sense of wonder at our ignorance of human potentiality and character.† François Truffaut, the French director who filmed the case, was struck by the cultural significance of the story and also by the "beauty of the theme"—the theme of two individuals educating one another for five years with devotion and resourcefulness. The Wild Boy had escaped from

---

* A team of psychologists recently trained an ape to use several words in sign language. In their documentary film, *The First Signs of Washoe*, they claim that their work destroyed "the last barrier of human uniqueness." Their experiment is far more valuable than this ill-founded conclusion.

† In a powerful mind like Darwin's, vast learning never stifled the capacity to marvel. During his voyage on the *Beagle* he wrote home from Chile: "But I have seen nothing which more completely astonished me than the first sight of a savage. It was a naked Fuegian, his long hair blowing about, his face besmeared with paint. There is in those countenances an expression which I believe, to those who have not seen it, must be inconceivably wild. Standing on a rock he uttered tones and made gesticulations, than which the cries of domestic animals are far more intelligible."

culture and sturdily resisted any return to it. The doctor believed equally sturdily in the power of culture to redeem from "wildness" and to confer humanity.

Both attained a form of greatness. Itard attained it by applying genuine talent to a challenging and worthwhile project. I believe the Wild Boy achieved greatness in the less recognized form of an ordinary or even lowly person who responds to exceptional circumstances in a way that exceeds our predictions and expectations. Though handicapped, he outdid himself and reached his limits. The Wild Boy belongs not to the history of genius but to the history of the species itself. He is the other prodigal, who did not squander his inheritance but, to a remarkable degree, recovered it after it had been taken from him. Helped and loved by Itard and Madame Guérin, the boy in his own modest way met the challenge expressed in Hamlet's lines that provide the epigraph for this book.

> . . . What is a man
> If his chief good and market of his time
> Be but to sleep and feed? A beast, no more.

Appendices

I

The Earliest Published Accounts

The first accounts of the Wild Boy in provincial newspapers have been lost. The earliest two articles to survive appeared in Paris publications. They contain so much of interest that I have translated them here in full.

Journal des débats et lois du pouvoir législatif (*Journal of Debates and Laws of the Legislative Branch*) was a semi-official magazine that survived many years of revolutionary politics and upheaval. It had a wide readership all over France. Nougairoles, the administrator of the orphanage in Saint-Affrique where the boy passed the first month after his capture, decided that this would be the appropriate place to announce the Wild Boy's case. He sent to the *Journal* Constans-Saint-Estève's letter of transmittal, along with a covering note of his own. They appeared on page 3 on January 24, 1800 (5 Pluviôse An VIII).

NEWS NOTES AND ANNOUNCEMENTS

True copy of the letter written January 10, 1800 (20 Nivôse An VIII) by the government commissioner in the

187

canton of Saint-Sernin to the administrative committee of the orphanage in Saint-Affrique.

Citizen:

I am sending to your orphanage an unidentified child twelve to fifteen years old who appears to have been born deaf and dumb. Beyond the interest inspired by his handicap, moreover, he displays in his behavior something extraordinary that places him in an almost savage state. In every respect this interesting and unfortunate being asks for the care of his fellow men; he might even attract the attention of a true philanthropist. I am informing the government of the case. It will no doubt decide that this boy should be entrusted to the celebrated and respected Sicard, the teacher of deaf-mutes.

Please have every care taken of the boy. Have him watched carefully during the day, and he should sleep in a room from which he cannot escape. In spite of the warm friendliness I have shown him, and even though I have won his confidence during the two nights and two days he has spent under close surveillance in my house, he remained on the lookout for an opportunity to escape. The food he ordinarily prefers since he has become a little civilized consists of potatoes cooked in the fire. When captured, he was feeding on roots and raw potatoes.

I shall send you without delay a detailed report on the circumstances that let him fall into my hands, on the conclusions I have reached about his way of life, and on the causes which must lead us to consider him a phenomenal creature.

> Greeting and esteem,
> Constans-Saint-Estève

The letter below, addressed to us by one of the administrators of the hospice in Saint-Affrique, furnishes details that will make up for the lack of the report promised by the commissioner.

Saint-Affrique, January 11, 1800

To the Editor:

I believe I should inform you, Citizen, of a phenomenon which has occupied all the inhabitants of this commune since this morning. Yesterday there was brought to our hospice, of which I am an administrator, a child who had originally been caught by three hunters in the woods near Lacaune. When they approached, he fled and climbed a tree. They took him to Lacaune, and he later escaped. He was caught again in some woods near Saint-Sernin and turned over to Constans-Saint-Estève, the commissioner. [*See letter above.*] The gendarmes who brought him here confirm that he had been captured as I have described. It is certain that he lives only on potatoes and nuts. If he is offered bread, he smells it, bites into it, spits it out, and throws it away. He acts the same with other foods. These facts leave no doubt that he lived for a long period in the woods. How did he survive the rigors of this winter in the Lacaune woods? It is the highest and coldest mountain of our region. The cold was worse this year than in 1795. The boy appears to be ten or twelve years old at most. He has an attractive face. His eyes are black and lively. He is constantly looking for a way to escape. This morning we let him out in a field next to the hospice. He ran off as fast as he could go. If someone hadn't chased him and caught him, he would have taken to the mountains and disappeared. He moves at a trot. A garment of gray cloth has been made for him, which he cannot get off. It bothers him a great deal. We have just put him out in the garden. He tried to get out by breaking the bars of the gate. He does not speak at all. When he is offered potatoes, he takes all his pretty little hands can hold. If they are cooked (he prefers them thus), he peels them and eats them like a monkey. He has a very agreeable laugh. When you take his potatoes away from him, he utters shrill cries. Constans thinks he is deaf; we have just convinced ourselves of the contrary. At most, he is a little hard of hearing. I shall let the scientists explain this phenomenon and make what they want of him. But I warmly hope that this interesting child will arouse the government's benevolent attention.

Nougairoles

We can date the Wild Boy's arrival in Paris exactly because of an anonymous article that appeared on August 8, 1800 (20 Thermidor An VIII), in the Paris newspaper *Gazette de France*. As was the practice then, many Paris newspapers and journals ran approximately the same article in their next issue. In a controversy that developed during the next few weeks about this "phenomenon," a crack-brained journalist named Feydel proclaimed that the boy was a charlatan free-loading on the government. Feydel also declared that Sicard was the author of the original article (translated below). Feydel may have been right, for in a terse letter rapping Feydel's knuckles Sicard does not quite disclaim authorship of the article. The promptness of the article, the information it contains, and the self-serving comments at the end of the first paragraph all suggest that Sicard was the author. Though hastily written, it raises almost all the significant questions about the case.

Savage of Aveyron

The child known by the name of the Savage of Aveyron, of whom the newspapers made so much six months ago, has been awaited in Paris with the impatience aroused by the memory of the Leblanc girl, also a savage, and by a few similar events now consigned to the records of various academies. This savage, about whom people had stopped talking because of his postponed arrival, finally arrived the day before yesterday, 18 Thermidor [August 6], at ten o'clock at night in the charge of an old serving man who has been caring for him for six months and of a professor of natural history at the Central School of Rodez, Citizen Bonnaterre. Yesterday the professor placed him in the hands of the Father of deaf-mutes, who received him as one more child in the interesting family created by his skill and devotion.

We still know very little about this child, who will now come under the observation of true philosophers. And he will no doubt be zealously visited by those who for a long time have wanted a child to be brought up apart from all social contact and communication, spoken to by no one, and whose tiniest actions could be watched such as he might use to express his first sensations, his first ideas and thoughts—if it is possible to *think* without fixed conventional signs. Such a child has now been found. Without our knowing yet whether or not he is a deaf-mute, he has so far uttered no articulate sound even to express his very limited needs. He uses only a few cries along with a few gestures and facial expressions. What is most astonishing is that, even though he spent a month in the hospice of Saint-Affrique, where he was treated like a beggar picked up on the highway and where no one observed his earliest behavior, he has not made a single step toward civilization and remains as far removed today from our customs and habits as he was the day he was found in a woods in Aveyron.

He is fairly well built, with an agreeable but slightly fleshy face. He is dressed like a three-year-old even though he looks to be about twelve, for he will not tolerate any other kind of clothing. His sheath-like garment is belted; having always refused them, he goes without shoes and stockings. He usually sits and sleeps on the ground or floor. It is only to please his old keeper, whom he seems to like very much, that he sits in a chair once in a while or consents to sleep in a bed. His preferred diet is potatoes, raw or cooked, and he eats them avidly; he also likes nuts. He dislikes meat; during the journey, however, he accepted a chicken wing. He will touch only dark bread. White bread seems to repel him, and he pushes away the hand that offers it. He is sometimes touched by the care people take of him and of his own accord holds out his hand to those who show an interest in him. But nothing can console him for the loss of his freedom and his earlier way of life, and he appears to want as much as ever to escape. He seems to hear the sound of a nut cracked behind him, yet he remains indifferent to all other noises. Although a few attempts were made in Saint-Affrique to teach him to speak, he says not a single word, not even a syllable.

We have Citizen Bonnaterre to thank for having kept him, if not in the purely savage state in which he was found, at least in the condition in which he left the hospice, which is almost the same. For, we repeat, he is as far removed from other men as the boy in the above-mentioned experiment would be. What a subject for reflection! For the time being, we will leave this vast terrain for our readers to survey!

This child spent eighteen days on the road because of various accidents that occurred. He came down with smallpox in Moulins. The illness was benign, and he arrived in Paris completely cured. When he arrived at Sicard's institute, he lay down on the ground and calmly went to sleep. Awakened shortly thereafter and touched by the interest shown in him by the teacher of deaf-mutes, he held out his hand with an affectionate air. He was offered bread, but it was white and he refused it, making a sign that he wanted to sleep. It turns out he is very tired and will be allowed to rest a few days before satisfying the curiosity that will surely be aroused in this city by so interesting a phenomenon.

II

Other Cases of Isolation and Deprivation

The Wild Boy's story stands on its own feet, casts its own shadow of meaning both in images and in words. It also occupies a place among a large number of related stories about men and women whose isolation from other human beings in some way modified their humanity. All these deprived persons suffered deeply. Some of them not only found their way to a full life but also turned out to be exceptionally warm and imaginative individuals. The six representative cases I shall discuss are not all familiar, but without exception they bear comparison with the Wild Boy's story.

The Castaway, or the Marooned Sailor

One night in 1708 an English privateer looking for Spanish prey off the coast of Chile spotted a fire on the uninhabited Juan Fernández Islands. The next day an armed party investigated and found, not a Spanish garrison, but a single white man with an overgrown beard and clad in goatskins. He turned out to be

British, as the captain recorded. "At his first coming on board us, he had so much forgot his language, for want of use, that we could scarce understand him, for he seemed to speak his words by halves. We offered him a dram, but he would not touch it, having drunk nothing but water since his being here." This was Alexander Selkirk, a thirty-year-old, headstrong Scottish sailor who had marooned himself four years before on the island after a quarrel with his captain. After an initial period of fear and melancholy, Selkirk had made an agreeable life for himself on the island and had remained in good health. The favorite illustration showing his island existence is based on another sentence in the captain's account: "He likewise tamed some Kids, and to divert himself would now and then sing and dance with them and his Cats."

In that era of heroic sea voyages, many tales were told of castaways. Selkirk's stands for them all because of the wide attention it received and because it furnished one of the possible sources for Defoe's *Robinson Crusoe*. When retold, Selkirk's story underwent startling changes. Some said he had reverted to an almost brutish state and totally lost his speech. For this reason he is frequently linked to the Wild Boy of Aveyron. Others liked to say that Selkirk resisted any return to the world outside his island kingdom. Several versions describe his deep religious meditations in the bosom of nature, meditations which presumably turned a rough simpleton into a wise and reflective creature of God, capable of becoming a good citizen when he returned to society. Defoe decided to have his shipwrecked sailor spend not four but *twenty-eight* years in solitude—except for Friday, who enters near the end of the narrative. Robinson Crusoe seems to have found a place in the collective human imagination. Simply and skillfully this first modern "novel" combined several elements: basic survival in the wilderness, getting away from the stresses of civilized life, preserving a few aspects of human culture, and solitary meditations on the place of man before God and in nature. It represents the kind of radical cure many of us think we would like to take.

The Romantics loved Defoe's book. The French writer and

philosopher Jean-Jacques Rousseau once wrote a startling sentence on the subject of education: "I hate books; they only teach people to talk about what they don't understand" (*Emile*). Yet he went on to recommend, ahead of everything else, "a complete treatise on Natural education"—namely *Robinson Crusoe.*

Peter of Hanover

Barely fifteen years after Selkirk's rescue, a very different case became the talk of London and the capitals of Europe. This time someone discovered, not an ordinary man who had partially reverted to nature, but a wild man "in the state of nature," who resisted any assimilation into human society. In a forest outside the town of Hamelin, near Hanover in Germany, residents captured a boy of about fourteen, reported to be naked, savage, and mute. Nine months later the boy, now baptized Peter, was taken to London, granted the special protection of King George I and his court, and assigned to the famous Dr. Arbuthnot to train. In 1726 a wave of pamphlets and satirical poems and serious articles swept London commenting on Peter's primitive life in the forest and the king's brief interest in him. Since Peter made little progress toward speech and caused no scandal, he was sent out to the country and lived to be more than seventy. Reports say he never developed any interest in either money or sex.

The discovery of abandoned children "gone wild" was not a rare event in Europe. Many fairy tales relate the terrible moment when the poor woodcutter and his wife must leave one or two children in the forest in order to save themselves and older children from starvation. Why then did Peter end up in London under the full barrage of publicity that could be mustered in 1726? It happened that King George I, the first of a new royal line in England, came from precisely the part of Germany where Peter had been found. George I could not even speak English! His was an almost home-town interest. Furthermore, at the beginning of the eighteenth century, naturalists and philosophers in many parts of Europe were becoming excited over the new science of anthropology—the study of man and why he is different from animals. Voyagers brought back amazing tales about savages, Hottentots, orangutans (often believed to be human), and children said to have been reared by animals. What they wanted to find most of all was a specimen of a human being "in the state of nature," the natural man. For a time Peter looked like the perfect case, the forbidden experiment, and by that time London had several weekly papers to trumpet the news. Defoe wrote a pamphlet called *Mere Nature Delineated* (1726) in which he raised all the essential issues. Had Peter really been "kept entirely from human society"? Was he happier than the rest of us for having been spared the corruption of other men? Could he be considered truly human if he had no words with which to think and communicate with others?

Peter's case fascinated another writer in London, Jonathan Swift. "This night I saw the wild Boy, whose arrival here hath been the subject of half our talk this fortnight . . . I can hardly think him wild in the Sense they report him." At this moment Swift was finishing *Gulliver's Travels*; the last section of the book describes the Yahoos, a race of near-beasts with a human anatomy. Disgusted by the Yahoos, who startlingly resemble the public image of Peter of Hanover, Gulliver attaches himself instead to some superior talking horses who can barely tolerate his Yahoo appearance. In Swift's wry upside-down fable about human animals and bestial men, Peter of Hanover entered literature even more rapidly than Selkirk.

Peter's case resembles that of the Wild Boy of Aveyron. But no one tried very hard to train Peter, and the circumstances of his isolation remain in doubt.

Kaspar Hauser

Unlike Peter of Hanover and the Wild Boy of Aveyron, Kaspar was not really wild. Historical circumstances linked him to mystery and scandalous crime in high places. Though obviously deprived of a normal youth, he was docile and good-natured from the start. Many authors have been moved by his story. The German movie version (called *Every Man for Himself and God against All*, by Werner Herzog) is a poetic and dramatic document utterly unlike Truffaut's film on the Wild Boy (see Appendix III).

Kaspar's story covers five years. Around five o'clock one spring afternoon in 1828 (the year of the Wild Boy's death), a grotesquely dressed boy of seventeen came staggering through the city gate of Nuremberg, Germany. Virtually speechless, he carried a letter from an unidentified person asking that he be given a place in the cavalry. Though he could mechanically write his name, the boy had the physical coordination and the mental responses of an infant. He accepted only bread and water and sat dully all day long on the floor playing with toy horses and drawing. He was so harmless that the town adopted him and put him under the care of a local teacher. Learned men and curiosity seekers came to visit this child-man. An eminent jurist, Anselm von Feuerbach, took a special interest and wrote a well-documented account concerned particularly with the legal aspects of Kaspar's case. The book's subtitle is "An Instance of a Crime against the Life of the Soul"—another way of phrasing the "forbidden experiment."

Kaspar made fairly rapid progress, learned rudimentary speech and the conventions of social living, and became a stickler for cleanliness and order. Especially at the start of his training, he had a prodigious memory for names and faces. He began to prefer certain colors, particularly red and white, and responded as passionately as the Wild Boy did to his first sight of snow. (Kaspar said the white paint had bitten him.) He always preferred indoors to out-of-doors and avoided bright light. He became a superb horseman. Finally his memory brought back the story of how he had spent years seated on the floor of a dark room, fed by a man who never spoke or let himself be seen, sealed off from any activity or stimulus. As Feuerbach said, "He slept through his childhood."

Those fragmentary revelations apparently frightened the person who had confined Kaspar and then released him. After one unsuccessful attempt on his life, Kaspar was murdered at twenty-two in a public park by an unknown man with a dagger. Much speculation surrounds the whole story. It appears that he may have been a pawn in a dispute over succession to the throne of Baden, and may also have been related to Josephine Bonaparte. Kaspar's probable connections with royalty redoubled the interest in his case. The mere fact that he had had a continuing relation to another human being—cruel though it was—explains why he was able to come a long way back toward the human condition. However, though Kaspar learned basic speech and even became curious about essentially philosophical problems of origin and causation, he never displayed much affection or any sexual feeling. When he spoke of marrying, he thought of a wife purely as a housekeeper. Like Peter and the Wild Boy, Kaspar was emotionally crippled for life.

The Elephant Man

Peter of Hanover, the Wild Boy of Aveyron, and Kaspar Hauser were all physically normal and psychologically deprived in different ways. The case of the Elephant Man provides a telling contrast with all three because it reverses the situation almost perfectly. We can easily sympathize with this unfortunate human being; yet his physical presence would probably repulse and terrify us.

Quite by chance, in 1884, a prominent English surgeon named Frederick Treves wandered into a run-down freak show on Mile End Road opposite London Hospital. There he found on display the most ugly, deformed, and degraded human being he had ever seen. The man had a totally misshapen head, a pink tusk or stump protruding out of his mouth from his upper jaw, one eye, and no real nose. The rest of him seemed to be all back and legs, with one withered arm and the other covered with a mass of brownish cauliflower skin in sacks. A terrible stench came from his body. Later this "Elephant Man" told Treves that he could never appear in public because the mere sight of him caused such consternation and terror that there were public disturbances. He could travel only in a black hood and at night. Treves wrote two medical papers on his condition, multiple neurofibromatosis, the same disease that Victor Hugo portrayed in Quasimodo.

A few years later the Elephant Man was abandoned on the Continent by his showman manager. He barely made his way alone back across the Channel to London without being mobbed. He had one thing in his pocket when the police picked him up: Treves's calling card. Out of sympathy and interest, Treves secured a tiny room for the man in an outbuilding of the London Hospital and found a way to get rid of the stench. There, as people got used to him as a genuine person named Merrick, he gradually came out of himself, showed a sensitive and pleasant disposition, and finally visited both the theater and the country. The Princess of Wales called on him and sponsored a subscription to support him. At the end of his life he became interested enough in improving his appearance to turn into something of a dandy—though he was still horrible to most eyes. Treves found a pretty young woman who had the courage to look him in the eye when she met him for the first time, smile, and shake his hand. Merrick wept—from his one eye. He told Treves, "I am happy every hour of the day." He died of suffocation when he tried to sleep stretched out on his bed like other people instead of curled up like an animal.

Treves wrote a beautiful account of Merrick's life, recently rediscovered by the anthropologist Ashley Montagu. The American author Bernard Pomerance adapted it as a successful and moving play. Unfortunately, Pomerance's play fails to bring out the miraculous side of the story: Why wasn't Merrick a disagreeable, embittered, and even dangerous monster? Why wasn't he retarded? Treves 'cannot emphasize the problem deeply enough. "It was not until I came to know Merrick was highly intelligent, that he possessed an acute sensibility and—worse than all—a romantic imagination, that I realized the overwhelming tragedy of his life." Yet tragedy is hardly the right word in spite of the hardship; and "worse" is an ironic adjective to apply to the imagination. Every day for years, this Elephant Man, who was both terrified of other human beings and ashamed of his own body, had to bear the humiliation of exhibiting himself in public. No one seemed to care for him, neither family nor state nor charity. He lived by degrading himself at the mercy of pitchmen. Yet this "monster" remained gentle and affectionate and bore no grudge—except possibly against the elephant which, he believed, had knocked his mother down while she was carrying him. His only possession in the world was a treasured portrait of his mother—an indication that he may have owed his sanity and his disposition to the fact that he had known genuine maternal love in his early childhood. He told Treves that he wanted to live in a lighthouse, or in an asylum for the blind. But he adjusted amazingly well to his existence as a kind of mascot for the hospital, and his presence brought out the best in most people. Considering the alertness and sensitivity of his mind, he must have suffered as few human beings are made to suffer. Yet he never seriously considered taking his own life.

Helen Keller

The life of Helen Keller cannot be told too often. Her own versions are by far the best, *The Story of My Life* as well as less-known and even moré resonantly poetic books like *The World I Live In* and *Teacher*. It took Anne Sullivan, a stranger aged twenty-one, only a few weeks to break and tame the uncontrollable vixen, Helen, aged seven. Anne's patience and kindness cannot be overestimated. Yet, under the circumstances, it is even harder to grasp the courage it must have taken for Anne to be cruel when necessary. For when Helen's refusal to be disciplined threatened to block any attempt at training, Anne dared to discipline her by tying her hands. This was equivalent to blindfolding her and stuffing her ears—or to shutting her away in a dark closet as Itard had done to the Wild Boy. And, as in the boy's case, nearly violent measures were needed to undo years of partial isolation.

It is hard to keep track of even the most basic facts of Helen Keller's astonishing life. She conversed as an equal with the great minds of the world—queens and presidents, artists and scientists. Mark Twain knew her well and admired in her "a new grace in the human spirit." Everything she knew she learned through her hands and fingers. She had to touch people's faces and bodies to "see" them, place her fingers on their lips to "hear" their words, and "listened" best to another person's fingers signing letters into her palm. She recognized people by shaking hands. She truly held hands with the world in an intimacy few of us begin to approach in ordinary living. Her dark silent world was so full of light and life and sure points of reference that she could swim and ride a bicycle, dance, go to the theater, take solitary walks in the woods, and shrewdly judge other people's character. One word often crops up in the best descriptions of her: *ardent.* She burned with the will and the capacity to be a full human being—not so much in spite of her handicaps as because of them.

All her life, Helen Keller existed in close physical touch with everything and everyone around her. The Wild Boy benefited from comparable physical contact only at the start of his training, in the form of massage and Madame Guérin's and Itard's affectionate fondling. But since he could see and hear normally, everyone expected him to stand on his own feet, use his senses, and live and communicate *at a distance.* In his film (see Appendix III), Truffaut conveys this alienation by showing the boy touching objects in his environment as he passes near them, in a constant confirmation of their reality.

Several other aspects of Helen Keller's life compare to what we know about the Wild Boy, even though he never became a whole person, as she did. Each as a child sank deep into a pit of loneliness; neither would have emerged without a dedicated and demanding teacher willing to risk failure and to spurn the easy response of pity. It is probably significant that the age difference was small in both cases: the teachers were fourteen years older than their pupils.

When they first saw the animal-like creatures they were to train, both teachers must have understood and accepted the fact that they would have to attempt total reeducation. Communication and knowledge lay on the far side of a process that had to begin with walking, sitting, dressing, eating, and obeying. Victor's progress in the first three months seems to have been as remarkable as Helen's in the first month—so much so that Itard deluded himself on the boy's future.

Most people are familiar with the scene that marked the great burgeoning of Helen Keller's life and that provides the most dramatic moment in the play *The Miracle Worker*, and in the film version. For months the young girl had no grasp of the meaning or purpose of the signs Anne Sullivan kept writing in her palm, even though she mimicked them and repeated them into her dog's paw. Then, suddenly one day by the pump, she understood that a symbol has a meaning. The comprehension came all at once, complete and unshaded, so that she immediately could learn all the words her memory could store. The understanding did not come in stages as is the case with a child, and as began happening with the Wild Boy. Unlike him, she struck no obstacles and never slipped back. Clearly she had better mental equipment than Victor. In any case she was several years younger and had never been abandoned as he had.

The most dramatic difference between the two stories is also the most obvious. It was Itard who wrote down the accounts of his pupil's long apprenticeship. Helen Keller, the pupil, wrote her own account, and also Anne Sullivan's, in a book appropriately called *Teacher*. We see Victor only from the outside. Helen Keller we see fully from outside and inside, for she was a great public figure observed and described everywhere she went, and a fine literary artist who seemed to treasure language as a special form of illumination in her great dark. She tells how she transcended her strong egotism and became passionately attached to ideals of beauty and love, justice and freedom. The poetic texture of her writing conveys an understanding of how this ardent and attractive woman, whose fingers moved intimately over the hands and faces of those around her, was able to transform her sensuousness into love for all mankind. Though she could never see or hear them, she developed a special sense for crowds and audiences in her public lectures. We can only imagine the Wild Boy's troubled egotism and his nascent emotions. He could never speak his mind or his heart as she could.

Genie

Isolation and deprivation we have always with us. Even the forms seem to remain similar. A very recent case, surrounded at the start by national publicity and legal dispute, recapitulates part of the Wild Boy's story along with an opening that recalls Kaspar Hauser. Genie's father was a successful machinist with an unstable personality who bullied his wife and two children into a life of almost total seclusion in their suburban home in California. Their only connection with the outside world was through the teenage son, who attended school and made the necessary purchases. During this period, the wife was going blind. The great change came when Genie was still an infant not yet two, normal except for a hip defect that made it difficult for her to walk. Partly because of this lameness and partially because of Genie's reaction to her father's beatings, he apparently decided that she was an incurably retarded child and "put her away" in their own house. Genie spent the next eleven years confined in a bare room with the door shut and the curtains drawn. One member of the family entered the room only long enough to feed her baby food. Since she had never been toilet-trained, she was strapped naked to a potty chair on the floor. Often she slept in this position; sometimes she was diapered, tied in a makeshift straitjacket, and placed in a crib. Because the father hated noise and even any communication (there was no radio or television in the house), Genie had almost no human contact, no toys, no change of routine, and only a few magazines to look at pictures in. Her father literally barked and growled at her from outside her door to scare her into silence, and beat her with a stick if she made any noise. This situation lasted until 1970, when the mother escaped from the house and took Genie with her. A social worker noticed the girl's condition. Television and newspapers made much of the story, and the parents were finally arrested. The day of the trial, the father committed suicide. At age thirteen Genie could not stand erect, walk, talk, chew solid food, or control her functions. Yet she was alert and fairly responsive to strangers. Her senses of sight and touch were highly developed; her hearing was blurred.

Placed for eight months in the rehabilitation center of a children's hospital, Genie developed fairly rapidly. In a sympathetic atmosphere of planned training, she soon learned to eat more normally, use the toilet, and walk—awkwardly, with the movements of a mannequin set in motion. Coordination of the simplest kind remained a great problem. Her sharp, pretty features wore a solemn yet impish expression till she laughed. Then the sound was shrill and unreal, as if she had never laughed or used her voice before. In the light of previous cases, particularly Victor's, everyone concerned with Genie's care wondered how she would develop.

Genie lived for three years as a foster child in a normal family situation with one of the doctors to whose charge she had been assigned. Other children her age played with her; she was expected to do her share in the household and to attend a special school. Gradually she developed her rudimentary sounds into basic utterances and could understand many more. But her language learning came to a stop at the level of a four- or five-year-old. It all required enormous effort on her part and on that of those training her. Today she lives in a home, under supervision. Genie is still "different"—socialized up to a point, unpredictable, not one of us. Her voice has never lost its unnatural quality, as if she were deaf. Only a few aspects of her intelligence—especially the visual and what we might call the aesthetic—continue to grow. Genie, then, made greater progress than the Wild Boy. Kaspar Hauser did better than either of them, yet something about all three remained inhuman.

Was it a question of the age at which they came back to society? Another case seems to support that possibility. A child found perfectly mute at the age of six because isolated with a mute mother attained normal speech within two years.

Naturally, Genie was given all kinds of tests—too many, some psychologists believe. Many were inconclusive, but a few of them revealed one unusual thing about the development of Genie's brain. I shall take a moment to explain. In recent years, scientists have worked out a theory that sounds like a refinement of Locke's and Condillac's *tabula rasa* or wax-tablet figure. Many experiments show that right-handed people learn language, mathematics, and logic with the left hemisphere of their brains, and do other kinds of thinking related to space, vision, and touch with the right hemisphere. Complex cross-circuitry connects the two sides. In left-handed individuals, the sides are reversed. This process of "lateralization" takes place during our early years, perhaps by the age of six—at least, before puberty. One theory proposes that once lateralization has been completed, a person is virtually unable to learn a first language. He must do so earlier. In other words, there is a "critical age" in our genetic code for learning certain skills, after which it is too late to learn them, or learn them fully. Experiments show that there is a critical age before which kittens must learn to see and avoid vertical obstacles; otherwise, they will never discriminate such objects and will bang into them. Experience and self-observation tell us that we learn many things much more easily when we are young than later in life.

Genie, like the Wild Boy, was discovered at puberty. Tests revealed that lateralization had taken place—but only the right hemisphere had developed. It seemed to fulfill all functions for her. Yet she was right-handed, a fact that would normally point to favoring the left hemisphere. As the theory would lead one to predict, her judgment of space relations was far better than her handling of sequential relations that we use to arrange words into sentences. Like Victor, she soon reached a plateau in language learning. Both learned a good number of words but could arrange them only in very elementary patterns. The fact that both of them learned a little language appears to reinforce rather than undermine the critical-age theory. It begins to look as if one plausible result of prolonged isolation in children might be restriction of mental development to one hemisphere, even in children "normal" at birth, and a stunting of the capacity to learn speech after this abnormal lateralization.

All this amounts to saying that Victor and Genie probably suffered irreversible functional brain damage from isolation. Yet we should never forget that the impaired mental organization they did achieve was effective enough to allow them to survive many years in a hostile environment without psychosis, autism, or lasting viciousness. And no matter how "wild" they had become, they responded immediately to treatment and regained a kind of partial humanity. The human mind appears to have a wonderful sturdiness and resiliency.

I have chosen to summarize these six cases because they supply a perspective that allows us to see the Wild Boy's story both as belonging to a rough category (severe deprivation by isolation from society) and as unique within that category. Lively and reliable accounts of all six individuals are available.

I should also mention a few other cases frequently associated with the Wild Boy's story. A little over fifty years ago, a Christian missionary in India discovered and captured two "wolf girls" aged about eight and one and a half. Local residents believed the girls had been nursed and reared by wolves. The older one survived to live nine years in the mission's orphanage and slowly changed from a nocturnally howling beast on all fours into an awkwardly erect, obedient, retarded girl. But there is a great deal of doubt about the authenticity of those "wolf girls."

Much has been written about Ishi, "the last wild Indian in North America," who in 1911 "wandered into the Modern World out of the Stone Age" and was befriended and protected by two young anthropologists. Ishi's is an authentic and fascinating case, as he was the last living member of the Yahi tribe in California and almost untouched by the white man's culture. It is essential to insist here that Ishi was in no sense "wild"; he was wild only in the eyes of a few arrogant Westerners who looked down on primitive peoples. For Ishi needed no taming or instruction. He represented a fully developed society with an integrated culture and language that had survived for centuries in a difficult environment. Indeed, this Yahi lived out his life literally in a museum, instructing admiring visitors in the techniques of his culture and in the wisdom of the Yahi religion. Ishi was not a wild man but a survivor.

In an unsettling book called *The Mountain People* (1972), Colin Turnbull, an English anthropologist, describes living with an African tribe, the Ik, whose traditional hunting habitat had been closed by a new government. As a result, their economic, social, and cultural system had broken down. That disintegration deprived the Ik of any firm collective basis for moral standards like mutual aid, decency, honesty, reliability. One devastating example of the breakdown was the practice of turning children out of the parental hut at the age of three or four to fend entirely for themselves. These children either perished or survived at a nearly bestial level of predatory behavior. *The Mountain People* gives one an uneasy sense of the precariousness of our social structures in the face of any traumatic disruption of our physical environment.

The Ik seem to have fallen away from what we think of as the essentials of humanity: respect for human life, continuity of generations, and some form of shared belief. As Itard kept repeating, human beings without culture are no better than beasts. Then what about attributing some form of culture to beasts? Many animals already have highly structured societies. In recent years, experimenters have trained a few specimens of the higher primates to respond to challenges in ways that suggest that their mentalities may be closer to ours than we have acknowledged in the past. Chimpanzees and other anthropoid apes have been taught to paint, to use rudimentary sign language, and to manipulate crude computers. Those apes appear in some cases to have come close to the level of intelligence and communication attained by Victor and Genie. Porpoises have responded to similar training. Here lies a whole world of fascinating lore (sometimes highly comical, especially when filmed), about which excessive claims are often made. We do not yet have to modify our classification of the species. But we will have to be very careful about how we distinguish abstract, fully symbolic language from signaling, mimicking, and trained responses.

The stories I have alluded to here concern the variety of forms that turn up on the outer edges of the domain called mankind. Most of us live within the middle range of human experience, yet we need some knowledge of the further limits. These cases, especially those of extreme isolation and deprivation, are like special mirrors that reveal hidden parts of our own humanity and animality.

III

The Wild Boy in Film

Except for a very few portraits, some faithful, some totally fanciful, the Wild Boy's story has come down to us in words. They tell it vividly. If discovered today, the Boy of Aveyron would surely be photographed and filmed around the clock. In this camera age we yearn for pictures, above all for *moving* pictures, which seem not merely to tell a story but to embody its luminous and living presence. It was inevitable that film directors would come upon the case of the Wild Boy. We can be grateful for the fact that the first of them to film the story was also among the best, and his film is worth examining as a sensitive modern commentary on the events.

François Truffaut belongs to the so-called New Wave of French film directors that emerged in the sixties. Many of them tended to eliminate the story line and to present vivid fragments of experience for the viewer to fit together himself. Truffaut has followed an independent course and often portrays people who live on the margins of society. His best-known films are *The 400*

Blows, Shoot the Piano Player, and *Jules and Jim.* Early in his career, Truffaut stated that what he wanted most was to make a film for children. Immediately after he saw *The Miracle Worker,* the play about Helen Keller, he cabled New York for the film rights, but he was too late by a few weeks. Later he read a review of a book about wild children, and that book led him to Itard's reports. Truffaut knew he had found his subject. Since he himself was virtually an abandoned child, rescued from wandering the streets of Paris by a film critic, he came to the story with strong sympathies. Truffaut's 1970 film, *The Wild Child (L'Enfant sauvage),* is an intelligent tribute to the human drama played out between a savage boy and a cultivated doctor.

Truffaut decided to make a "barely fictionalized" historical film. By choosing to shoot in black and white instead of in color and to use little-known actors rather than stars, he kept the action soberly focused on the events as Itard told them. The choice of actors was particularly difficult. After rejecting a series of stage-struck boys in Paris for the role of Victor, he sent one of his assistants to several towns in southern France. There she photographed boys as they came boiling into the street after school. One boy in Montpellier struck them as looking and acting the part of a child of the forests. He turned out to be a gypsy, Jean-Pierre Cargol, son of a famous guitarist.

But who would play Itard? In much of the film, the doctor has the role of "directing" Victor to "act" like a civilized person. While trying out various actors, Truffaut found himself directing them how to direct the boy, and that seemed clumsy. Finally he found it was far simpler and more natural to direct the boy himself, "in front of the camera," as he said. This decision also saved money in a tightly limited budget of $400,000. Truffaut became an actor for the first time in his career in order to direct the Wild Boy on camera. Since the narrative of the film consists of selections from Itard's reports, Truffaut reads them also. And when an English version of the film was made, he dubbed the narrative himself, with an appropriate French accent. It is a very personal work.

The press was not comfortable with the film when it was released, or with Truffaut's switch from modern fictional subjects to a documentary about a hundred-and-fifty-year-old case history. Many critics found the film warm and convincing; others called it dull and pretentious. Wide attention in the newspapers never settled the question whether it was "moving" or "inept." The film broke no box-office records, but it continues to be shown all over the world in schools and to special audiences.

To tell the Wild Boy's story in eighty-five minutes of picture and sound required vigorous and imaginative telescoping. The six months the boy spent in Rodez simply disappear, along with patient, enterprising Father Bonnaterre. Truffaut makes no attempt to present the political and social upheavals that are the framework for the Wild Boy's appearance. The chronology of events once the boy arrives in Paris is similarly condensed. Where Itard summarized, Truffaut slashed. Yet he preserved the essential flavor of the story.

The power of the film grows out of Truffaut's grasp of the basic situation, the remarkable family unit of Victor, Itard, and Madame Guérin. The freak-show elements do not take over. The boy is twelve years old at the start, yet almost everything is happening to him for the first time as if he were an infant. We witness his first sneeze, his first tears, his first pair of shoes, his first spoken word. This refrain running through the film reminds us to look again at what we take for granted, to rediscover the familiar. Victor is coming to life, and for Cargol's lithe body Truffaut imagined a whole repertory of animal-like movements, some of them derived from the behavior of autistic children. In the film the boy at the beginning is almost on all fours and gradually becomes erect. Like a cat, he continues to rub against and touch many of the objects in his environment. His eye responses develop from distracted blinking into a quiet, attentive gaze. In the early scenes he rocks, cradles himself, crouches, and makes disturbing spastic movements. Later he moves almost normally, though always restless.

Opposite Cargol, Truffaut plays Itard as calm and firm, a

man at home in his culture and yet detached from it. He never shows distress or passion, and keeps writing soberly his daily account of the training program. What he is writing are key passages from Itard's reports. By reading them "voice over" while he scratches away with a quill pen, Truffaut keeps the scientific, case-history tone even where Itard's prose becomes personal or sentimental. Madame Guérin has the most human part, a simple, understanding woman willing to dedicate herself to an almost inhuman boy. The film restores her to a central role sometimes passed over or taken for granted in the reports. Without her warm heart, the film would not be believable.

Truffaut's sober black-and-white images create such a convincing version of the story that it is already a nearly definitive account in the public mind. Yet a person familiar with the events as they actually occurred will be aware of certain liberties Truffaut took in his adaptation. For example, throughout his years of training, Victor lived in the Institute for Deaf-Mutes in a room above Madame Guérin's. Itard had his own apartment in another wing. Victor, therefore, was often surrounded by gesticulating, grunting deaf-mute boys (and, for a few years, girls), whom he never learned to get along with. Furthermore, life at the institute was very uncomfortable, and sometimes miserable, in those uncertain times. (A number of shots at the beginning of the film show the institute, little changed today from its appearance in 1800.) Truffaut changes those historical circumstances by having Itard live in a private house in the country with Madame Guérin as his housekeeper. In the film, the Wild Boy soon leaves the institute to stay with them. This departure from historical events was forced on Truffaut because he could set up his equipment in the institute only for a few days, and because he had to find a setting remote from Paris noise in order to use direct sound rather than post-synchronization. The film presents this altered version of the events so convincingly that some unwary scholars have accepted it as fact. Yet the reports show how hard it was to separate Victor from the surrounding distractions of the institute in order to get his attention. The process of awakening took place in the midst of the comings and goings of a busy, over-crowded, poverty-stricken institution that housed four hundred boarders. The sequences Truffaut shows us in and around Itard's country house look like life in the garden of Eden. The lovely Vivaldi music occasionally used on the sound track reinforces this lyric effect.

Several other sequences in the film depart from the true events. When Victor began to resist learning the cutout letters by throwing temper tantrums and becoming almost hysterical, Itard shocked him out of this behavior pattern by extreme fright. The scene lends itself to effective film treatment, yet Truffaut never shows us Itard dangling the boy out the fifth-story window (see pages 103–5). Instead, in the film version, the doctor shuts the boy in a closet. The extreme shock effect is lost, along with circumstances that have psychiatric significance. (Truffaut has written me that he no longer remembers why he changed the scene; he may have found it "excessive.") Furthermore, Itard's account indicates that the boy was desperately afraid of heights, even though there is some evidence that he climbed trees with ease. In an early sequence in the film, Truffaut shows the boy climbing to the top of a huge tree and rocking in his perch as he looks out over the forest. It makes an unforgettable shot of the boy in his "wild" environment. But if, in order to keep it, Truffaut decided to change acrophobia to claustrophobia in the later shock-therapy scene, he sacrificed authenticity at the wrong point.

There is another serious difference between Itard's account and the film. Itard leaves no doubt that one of the principal reasons why Victor's training could not go on was that the boy did not know how to direct his developing sexual responses toward any particular object. He had no idea of "the other sex," and Itard did not find a way to instruct him. Itard discreetly yet emphatically tells us that the boy's immodesty and the onset of puberty posed insuperable problems that no one had adequately foreseen. Truffaut passes over the whole question. Sex does not exist in the film.

Even though Truffaut uses details and scenes from both Itard's reports, he shapes his material to cover only the first nine months of the boy's training. Near the end of the film, Itard is shown writing the closing words of his *first* report. Accordingly the tone is hopeful. In the film, when Victor comes back of his own accord after running away (the spontaneous return is Truffaut's invention), Itard can speak with a glow of feeling about the boy's "great expectations." The last words of the film imply more work ahead and a happy outcome: "Soon we'll begin our exercises again." Ending the account on this optimistic note, without any reference to the slowing down of progress over the following five years, distorts the basic outline of the story as it really happened. It transforms a true account of courage and humanity in the face of insuperable obstacles into an amputated semi-fiction. We do not get the whole truth.

I believe it is worth quoting in full Truffaut's thoughtful response to the above paragraph after he saw it in manuscript.

> I don't regret having ended the film on a hopeful note, since Victor had actually learned a number of things and words. But I willingly admit that after the last scene, exactly as I did in *The Story of Adele H.*, I should have added an illustrated narrative of what happened to the characters after we leave them on the screen.   —Letter dated April 26, 1979

Despite its flaws, Truffaut's adaptation belongs to a class totally apart from several painfully bad versions that have been made recently for television. The New Wave director did not shrink from conveying Itard's fundamental message: without other human beings around him in his formative years, an individual human being comes to nothing, remains abject. Truffaut also underscored two other points. Some form of communication in language is essential for the development of social bonds. And often one must cause pain in order to help another person, as when we use discipline. *The Wild Child* is a beautiful and moving film. It contains fine shots of Victor lured outside at night by a full moon, and later cavorting in a pelting rain that any civilized person would avoid. But the most unforgettable image is of the boy fleeing across a brightly lit, cultivated field back toward an awesome black area of woods that gradually fills the screen like an impenetrable wall. This time, unlike the opening, nature looks forbidding, and the basic theme of the film is portrayed in a stunning composition in black and white.

Further Reading and Sources

The Wild Boy and Itard

Itard's reports of 1801 and 1806 are available in English in an inexpensive but unreliable version: *The Wild Boy of Aveyron,* translation by G. Humphrey and M. Humphrey (New York: Appleton-Century-Crofts, 1932). The original French texts can be found in Lucien Malson's *Les Enfants sauvages* (Paris: 10/18, 1964), translated as *Wolf Children and the Problem of Human Nature* (New York: Monthly Review Press, 1972). Malson's chapters on the "myth and reality" of wild children are informative, and his bibliography includes many items in English.

The case and Itard's whole career are carefully examined in Harlan Lane's *The Wild Boy of Aveyron* (Cambridge: Harvard University Press, 1976). On pages 33–48, Lane gives a translation of the essential section of Bonnaterre's book, *Notice historique sur le Sauvage de l'Aveyron* (1800), along with passages from Virey's *Dissertation* (1800). Lane's twenty-four-page bibliography is close to exhaustive. One caution: Lane, like Truffaut in his film, mistakenly has Itard removing Victor from the Institute for Deaf-Mutes to train him in his own home. See my review in *The New York Times Book Review,* May 16, 1976.

A brief discussion of the case appears in Bruno Bettelheim's

215

The Empty Fortress: Infant Autism and the Birth of the Self
(New York: The Free Press, 1967).

The best-informed and most perceptive investigator working
on the subject today is Thierry Gineste, a French psychiatrist
attached to the Hôpital de Villejuif, just outside Paris. His most
recent article (written in association with a prominent psychiatrist and historian of psychiatry) cites many new documents, refers
to earlier articles, and presents the full story in the most respected
French journal in the field: Th. Gineste and J. Postel, "J. M. G.
Itard et l'enfant connu sous le nom de 'Sauvage de l'Aveyron,'"
La Psychiatrie de l'enfant, vol. XXIII (1980). Gineste has published
all documents pertinent to the case with a long introduction in
Le Sauvage de l'Aveyron: aux origines de la psychiatrie française
(Paris: Sycomore, 1981).

Related Cases

The basic facts on John Selkirk appear in Daniel Defoe's
Robinson Crusoe, edited by Michael Shinagel (New York: W. W.
Norton, 1975).

On Peter of Hanover, I recommend Maximillian E. Novak's
"The Wild Man Comes to Tea," in Edward Dudley and Maxi-
millian E. Novak, editors, *The Wild Man Within* (Pittsburgh:
University of Pittsburgh Press, 1972).

The original text on Kaspar Hauser is by the man who studied
the case firsthand, Paul J. Anselm von Feuerbach. It exists in
various editions.

Ashley Montagu's *The Elephant Man: A Study in Human
Dignity* (New York: Outerbridge and Dienstfrey, 1971) is among
the most readable and touching of all these accounts. See also
Bernard Pomerance's *The Elephant Man* (New York: Grove Press,
1979).

Helen Keller's *The Story of My Life* (1905) deserves the wide
reading it enjoys in high schools. *The World I Live In* (1908) is
an even wiser and better-written book. It is a shame that this
work and most of her other writings receive little attention and

have gone out of print. See also the straightforward and sympathetic short biography by Van Wyck Brooks, *Helen Keller: Sketch for a Portrait* (New York: E. P. Dutton, 1956).

On Genie, a fairly technical book is available: Susan Curtiss's *Genie: A Psycholinguistic Study of a Modern Day "Wild Child"* (New York: Academic Press, 1977).

Two accounts of the Wolf Children of India appeared forty years ago: Arnold Gesell's *Wolf Child and Human Child* (New York: Harper and Brothers, 1941), and J. A. L. Singh and Robert M. Zingg's *Wolf Children and Feral Man* (New York: Harper and Brothers, 1942). Those accounts were reexamined and thrown into serious doubt by William F. Ogburn and Mirmal K. Bose's "On the Trail of the Wolf Children," *Genetic Psychology Monographs*, Vol. 60 (1959), pp. 117–93. A later book partly rehabilitates the story: Charles Maclean, *The Wolf Children* (New York: Hill and Wang, 1978).

The Ik tribe is described by Colin Turnbull in *The Mountain People* (New York: Simon and Schuster, 1972).

Ishi: A Biography of the Last Wild Indian in North America is by Theodore Kroeber (Berkeley: University of California Press, 1961).

One cannot list these books on recorded case histories without mentioning Kipling's *The Jungle Book* (1894). The opening stories concern Mowgli, a fictional wolf-boy who lives on the alluring and dangerous frontier between the animal and the human.

We know very little about the "Lost Woman of San Nicolas," a kind of female Robinson Crusoe. At the age of twelve she remained behind on an island in the Pacific off Los Angeles when her tiny Indian tribe abandoned it in 1835. Scott O'Dell based a young people's novel on the situation: *Island of the Blue Dolphins* (New York: Houghton Mifflin, 1960).

Other Works

Bernheimer, Richard: *Wild Men in the Middle Ages: A Study in Sentiment and Demonology* (Cambridge: Harvard University

Press, 1952; New York: Octagon Books, 1970). Scholarly, full of fascinating lore.

Bowlby, John: *Attachment* (New York: Basic Books, 1969). A fundamental study of human development and our need for other people during early stages.

Brown, Roger: *Words and Things* (Glencoe: The Free Press, 1968). A lively book on language and thinking.

Lenneberg, Eric H.: *Biological Foundations of Language* (New York: John Wiley & Sons, 1967). A basic book on how we learn language, and its relation to thought.

Piaget, Jean: *The Language and Thought of the Child,* translated by Marjorie Gobain (New York: Meridian Press, 1955; original publication, 1924). Contains wonderful case histories.

Rousseau, Jean-Jacques, *Discours sur l'origine et les fondements de l'inegalité parmi les hommes,* 1755. Available in many English translations, sometimes as *The Second Discourse*. A seminal text on social theory, with a discussion of wild children and the "state of nature."

Acknowledgments

This book grew out of a series of lectures and seminars in high schools, sponsored by the National Humanities Faculty in 1972 and 1973. Whenever possible, I showed the Truffaut film *The Wild Child* (1970), where I first encountered the story. Since no readable account of the case existed in English, teachers and students urged me to develop these materials into a book. During a three-year period of residence in Vermont, I received a travel grant to France from the American Philosophical Society and some much needed support from the Salk Institute in La Jolla, California. Jacob Bronowski, of the Salk Institute, encouraged my work on the project until his death in 1975. His assistant, Harry Boardman, continued that interest, and administered some vigorous prodding.

Through Bronowski and Boardman I met Harlan Lane, a psycholinguist who had been working for a number of years in Paris on the same subject. His substantial study (see "Further Reading and Sources") is quite different in purpose and scope

219

from my narrative account. Lane graciously supplied copies of many documents I lacked.

Thierry Gineste, the French psychiatrist and scholar, has been most cordial in bringing to my attention new materials he discovered while preparing his thesis for a degree in psychiatry. To his devotion I also owe the illustrations. Our correspondence contributed significantly to the last stages of my writing.

M. Bernard, archivist and librarian at the Institution Nationale des Jeunes Sourds de Paris, and Jean Delmas, director of the Archives Départementales de l'Aveyron, helped me locate documents and answered many questions. The staff of the Middlebury College Library was attentive to my needs during the years when I resided nearby.

Dr. Ursula Bellugi, Dr. Gaston Ferdière, Dr. Louis Gayral, Lucien Malson, Dr. David Rigler, René Glises de la Rivière, and François Truffaut have graciously supplied information and discussed my project. I am grateful to several individuals who read and criticized the manuscript at various stages: Dore Ashton, Robert Bernstein, Lester Crocker, Paul Schmidt, Mary Lee Settle, Edna Shapiro, Victor Turner, and several loyal Shattucks (Patricia, Petra, Ruth, and Tari). My wife has found ways to give special support to this slow-ripening book.

Lincoln, Vermont, 1973
Charlottesville, Virginia, 1978